THE
UNIVERSALITY OF GOD'S MERCIES:
THE
BOOK OF JONAH

Isaac O. Ajibolorunrin

Grosvenor House
Publishing Limited

This book is published by
Grosvenor House Publishing Ltd
Link House
140 The Broadway, Tolworth, Surrey, KT6 7HT.
www.grosvenorhousepublishing.co.uk

A CIP record for this book
is available from the British Library

Paperback ISBN 978-1-83615-470-9
eBook ISBN 978-1-83615-471-6

DEDICATION

This book is dedicated to all our brethren at Christ The Lord Tabernacle worldwide. All the glory be to God!

CONTENTS

ACKNOWLEDGEMENTS

The foundation of this book originated from one of my doctorate research projects titled, The Abundant Mercies of God towards Jonah. Thank you, Professor Clinton L. Ryan (Professor of Divinity for Canada Christian College School of Graduate Theological Studies), for being the inspiration behind the project without knowing at the time that it would become the gem of this book.

I extend my sincere appreciation to all the members of Christ the Lord Tabernacle, and everyone connected to our Church for good.

And to my beautiful wife Esther, and adorable Alice, thank you for all you do, and your sacrifices in God's vineyard. God bless you.

The most important of all, I wholeheartedly give thanks and praise to God for this publication, He deserves all the glory.

FOREWORD

It is both a great honour and privilege to write the foreword to this inspiring book. Pastor Isaac O. Ajibolorunrin has been my prayer partner for over a decade, and during this time, I have been consistently impressed by his passion for the Word of God, his profound reverence for Him and his deep knowledge of biblical truth, which he communicates so powerfully during our daily prayers.

This book is yet another testimony to his calling. It confirms, without doubt, that the Bible remains the sure foundation for human growth, renewal and sanity. More than a resource, it is an inspiration. Pastor Isaac takes the profound theme of the Universality of God's Mercies: The Book of Jonah, and presents it in a way that is practical, engaging and accessible to all.

What makes this work particularly remarkable is Pastor Isaac's unique ability to weave together research, spiritual insight, and real-life application. His counsel and biblical expositions have personally helped me grow as a true son of the Most High, bringing strength in my moments of trial and joy in my seasons of celebration.

Indeed, the mercies of God, as revealed throughout Scripture, are abundant and beyond human description.

I wholeheartedly recommend this book. Whether you are encountering this subject for the first time or are already well-versed in it, you will discover fresh insights that will enrich your walk with God. The pages ahead will expand your understanding, stir your faith and challenge you to take meaningful steps in your spiritual journey.

God bless you richly as you read.

Sir Olu Okeowo
Founder & Chairman Gilbratar Construction Nigeria Ltd
Lagos, Nigeria

INTRODUCTION

God's mercies abound all over the Bible, but I will limit my writing to the type of mercy shown by God in Jonah's life through the latter's book. He was sent to evangelise the Ninevites, to call them to repentance and allow God to take the credit. Was it a straightforward missionary duty, or more would be required from God before Jonah would act? Personally, I have always benefited variously from God's mercies long before I wrote this book, but this publication has brought me to another dimension which has deepened my understanding about the universality of God's mercies— Jonah had problem with that at the beginning.

Indeed, the vastness of God's mercies towards me is indescribable. So many times and at different occasions one came close to death, but through God's mercies I have been preserved. When it was time to answer the Call into Ministry, although I did not run away like Jonah, but I was reluctant, hesitant and gave God many excuses until He said, "Enough!" It was after that encounter that I accepted the call. From my personal view, I would say, do not blame Jonah because you do not know his personal circumstance prior, especially, before he was instructed to go to Nineveh for the missionary task.

Notwithstanding, we have a lot to learn from this book, it is for every Christian believer and everyone aspiring to walk in obedience to God's bidding, and looking for His mercy. It is a volume that will help you to appreciate how God has been merciful and compassionate towards you—much more than you thought. And importantly, it is a book that shows that,

God can be merciful to the outcast and the undeserved, and He wants you to be merciful and compassionate to your fellow humans universally, no matter who they are, and where they come from. For short, it is a book that shows the universality of God's mercies—join me on this journey of discovery.

Reverend Dr Isaac Ajibolorunrin

CHAPTER ONE
THE GENEALOGY OF JONAH

Was He A Real Person?

Jonah was the son of Ammittai of Gath-hepher (Jonah 1:1) which belongs to the tribe of Zebulun. Who was Zebulun and who were the tribe of Zebulun? Zebulun as an individual was one of the twelve sons of Jacob and it was through him that the tribe of Zebulun came about. Sequentially, Zebulun was the tenth son out of Jacob's twelve children, (Genesis 30:20). But the sixth son of Leah the sister of Rachel who were both married to Jacob.

> And Leah said, "God has endowed me with a good endowment; now my husband will dwell with me, because I have borne him six sons." So she called his name Zebulun. Genesis 30:20

It must be emphasised that despite being sisters, there was a matrimonial rivalry between Leah and Rachel, in regards to who Jacob their husband should love more. Without any doubt, Jacob loved Rachel more than Leah, (Genesis 29:16). The background story in (Genesis 29:16-25), will help you to understand better.

> Now Laban had two daughters: the name of the elder was Leah, and the name of the younger was Rachel. 17 Leah's eyes were delicate, but Rachel was beautiful of form and appearance. 18 Now Jacob loved Rachel; so he said, "I will serve you seven years for Rachel your

younger daughter." 19 And Laban said, "It is better that I give her to you than that I should give her to another man. Stay with me." 20 So Jacob served seven years for Rachel, and they seemed only a few days to him because of the love he had for her. 21 Then Jacob said to Laban, "Give me my wife, for my days are fulfilled, that I may go in to her." 22 And Laban gathered together all the men of the place and made a feast. 23 Now it came to pass in the evening, that he took Leah his daughter and brought her to Jacob; and he went in to her. 24 And Laban gave his maid Zilpah to his daughter Leah as a maid. 25 So it came to pass in the morning, that behold, it was Leah. And he said to Laban, "What is this you have done to me? Was it not for Rachel that I served you? Why then have you deceived me?" Genesis 29:16-25

The Bible records that Rachel who was originally meant to be the first wife of Jacob, was deceivingly denied him by Laban. The Lord will send all fraudulent people away from your life permanently, in the name of Jesus Christ. Again, for all your God-ordained enterprise, you will not be robbed. Way forward, Jacob served Laban for another seven years to marry Rachel, in total making fourteen years. My prayer for you is that, you will not need to work twice the normal effort before you earn your dreamed trophy.

Meanwhile, Leah had already been given in marriage to Jacob by Laban in what appeared to be a deceptive switch. This foul-play made Rachel to become the second wife as we read in (Genesis 29:18-25). As time went on, there was a contention and unusual rivalry between the two sisters who were married to their husband (Jacob). A statement of reference to show there was a marital competition is as remarked in (Genesis 30:15),

But she said to her, "Is it a small matter that you have taken away my husband? Would you take away my son's mandrakes also?" And Rachel said, "Therefore he will lie with you tonight for your son's mandrakes." Genesis 30:15

One wonders if the mandrakes were meant to grant access to the matrimonial bed for the time being, or a customary bargaining between the two of them for the right to sleep with Jacob if they were taking turns. It was shortly after the above conversation that Zebulun was born as narrated in (Genesis 30:17-20),

And God listened to Leah, and she conceived and bore Jacob a fifth son. 18 Leah said, "God has given me my wages, because I have given my maid to my husband." So she called his name Issachar. 19 Then Leah conceived again and bore Jacob a sixth son. 20 And Leah said, "God has endowed me with a good endowment; now my husband will dwell with me, because I have borne him six sons." So she called his name Zebulun. Genesis 30:17-20

As stated above, it was through this sixth son that the tribe of Zebulun come from. One day when Jacob realised he would die soon, he called all his sons for prayers and he gave some prophetic parting words over them. Even though it was a last testament of Jacob, (Zebulun's earthly father), it was prophetic as it turned out to be perfectly true later in the lives of the people of that tribe. In a nutshell, Zebulun was described by his father (Jacob) as a tribe that would be located where they would engage in sea trade and gain prominence in commerce as expressed in (Genesis 49:13),

Zebulun shall dwell by the haven of the sea; He shall become a haven for ships, And his border shall adjoin Sidon. Genesis 49:13

What Happened To The Prophecy?

No one imagined that many years later among their future generation, there would be a person called Jonah who would be involved with traders and sailors. Further, they wouldn't have believed that God at a point in history would send an individual called Jonah to travel by sea to Nineveh on a missionary duty which turned out to be a spectacular assignment.

Again, it would have been inconceivable to them if they were told that years to come, they would be allocated a landed inheritance as a tribe (Zebulun) in the Promised Land. As biblically indicated, their landed allocation which comprised of some of the most fertile land in the Plain of Jezreel was prophetically uttered by their forefather (Jacob).

My prayer for you is that, you will inherit generational blessings and not curses in the name of Jesus Christ. It is sad to say, but it is worth mentioning that, presently many people are labouring under the curse of what their fathers or forefathers did. May God who delivered the Israelites through His outstretched arm, deliver you completely, and all your loved ones in the name of Jesus Christ. May He show you His lovingkindness always, and throughout your lifetime, (Jeremiah 32:16-18). Let us read,

"Now when I had delivered the purchase deed to Baruch the son of Neriah, I prayed to the LORD, saying: 17 'Ah, Lord GOD! Behold, You have made the heavens and the earth by Your great power and outstretched arm. There is nothing too hard for You. 18 You show lovingkindness to thousands, and repay the iniquity of the fathers into the bosom of their children after them—the Great, the Mighty God, whose name is the LORD of hosts. Jeremiah 32:16-18

Your case will not be difficult for God to solve in the name of Jesus Christ. The iniquity of the fathers will not hinder you. If God had shown His lovingkindness to many thousands in the past, He will remember you and include you in this season, amen.

Furthermore, when the Israelites entered the Promised Land, Joshua the son of Nun divided the land of Canaan to the Israelites and when the lot came up, the children of Zebulun received their inheritance as recorded in (Joshua 19:10-16). This explains the tribal or genealogical root of Jonah.

The Land Given to the Tribe of Zebulun: The third tribe to receive its assignment of land was Zebulun. Its boundary started on the south side of Sarid. 11 From there it circled to the west, going near Mareal and Dabbesheth until it reached the brook east of Jokneam. 12 In the other direction, the boundary line went east to the border of Chisloth-tabor, and from there to Daberath and Japhia; 13 then it continued east of Gath-hepher, Ethkazin, and Rimmon and turned toward Neah. 14 The northern boundary of Zebulun passed Hannathon and ended at the valley of Iphtahel. 15-16 The cities in these areas, besides those already mentioned, included Kattath, Nahalal, Shimron, Idalah, Bethlehem, and each of their surrounding villages. Altogether there were twelve of these cities. Joshua 19:10-16

Where Do We Go From Here?

In our quest for some more information about Jonah, as we progress in this remarkable exercise, we might ask some questions as listed below:

Did the Nineveh missionary duty really took place? Did the Nineveh missionary duty popularise Jonah? Was God being intentional about the genealogical root of this individual called Jonah? What made Jonah's bloodline to be significant in his assignment? Did any prophecy come true for the tribe of Zebulun? Where was Jonah before the Nineveh commission? For a more in-depth understanding and clarity, it is appropriate to discuss some of the attributes of Jonah's ministry in regards to the historical, social and political sentiments, or nuances of his days in the next chapter.

CHAPTER TWO
THE ATTRIBUTES OF JONAH'S MINISTRY

An Overview

The attributes of Jonah's ministry can be understood better when we consider some of the historical, social and political sentiments that were happening during his time. Also, it is important to bear in mind the prophecy that was uttered by Jacob on Zebulun who was Jonah's forefather, (Genesis 49:13).

> "Zebulun shall dwell by the haven of the sea; He shall become a haven for ships, And his border shall adjoin Sidon. Genesis 49:13

God can use anybody but on this missionary journey, He was ready to send someone who was accustomed to sea life and sea travel, and He found that person in Jonah, the son of Ammittai of Gath-hepher which belongs to the tribe of Zebulun. Again, it should be remembered that Jonah's missional journey to Nineveh was not his first assignment as we shall see later. Further, it is pertinent to find out if he (Jonah) was a human agent sent by God or not? And how does the Bible describe him? We shall come to this topic soon.

Villain or Angel

The reality of life is, you need one good person (angel) to help you and you are done, but it takes one ungodly person (villain) you allow into your 'ship' (life) to truncate the entire journey of destiny. Similarly, one villain on your Board of Directors/Trustees can frustrate your business or ministry. Further, it takes one evil adviser among your business associates to collapse your business, or a bad friend to break one's marriage, or a relationship and so on. My prayer is that, God will deliver you from known and unknown destroyers or villains. Wasters of time, resources, opportunities and glory shall not find you in the name of Jesus Christ. The Lord will send your way good people that will help you.

It is important to note that when Jonah was running away from God, so long as he was in the ship, advancement and speed were difficult to achieve by the voyagers because of the stormy wind which God had released against them. May God deliver you from every power militating against your progress in life, and I pray that your transition to the next level shall be with ease. From today you will not learn in a hard way any more.

The Historical And Political Enmity Between Israel And The Assyrians

The rationale behind Jonah's decision to go to Tarshish instead of Nineveh, and the resultant waste of merchandise was unacceptable. Even so, we should try and see the reason for his behaviour. Historically, the northern part of Israel which Jonah came from was exposed to Assyrian invasion, and the latter being their aggressor caused them a lot of pain, which naturally meant he (Jonah) would have disliked them for the atrocities and hardship they (the Assyrians) caused his people. As God's children we need to refrain from allowing our emotions or animosity to over-ride the ideals of God. You will be accountable for every action you take, good or bad. Let God fight for you or avenge your enemies whichever way He chooses. Only God does what He pleases (Psalm 135:5-6), you and I are not God, and so cannot do whatever we like.

> For I know that the LORD is great, And our Lord is above all gods. 6 Whatever the LORD pleases He does, In heaven and in earth, In the seas and in all deep places. Psalm 135:5-6

Also, remember God's instruction for His children is, love your enemies and do good to them as in (Luke 6:35), let us read,

> But love your enemies, do good, and lend, hoping for nothing in return; and your reward will be great, and you will be sons of the Most High. For He is kind to the unthankful and evil. Luke 6:35

Furthermore, Jonah was a prophet of God who was sent to go and deliver a message of repentance to an Assyrian capital city, and he owed his duty to God and had no right to do whatever he liked. But Jonah's attitude possibly was, "Why should God spare them when they are our aggressors? I won't go, let God judge or kill them—they are our enemies." However, God was thinking differently, unknown to Jonah who by now was disobeying God by going the opposite direction. I pray that people's behaviour will not make you to sin against God. Also, I pray that you will not misunderstand God in any circumstance you find yourself.

Jonah's Ministry Before Nineveh

God was not out to promote Himself or popularise any of His servants. But rather, He is Sovereign and does whatever He wants for the good of humanity. He does His things with good intentions and bears their eternal consequences at heart. God is not a politician, as we know, they (politicians) try to please the public in order to gain their votes when required. Not only that, politicians change and renege on their promises or manifestos, but God does not change, hear what is said about Him in (Malachi 3:6),

> For I am the LORD, I do not change; Therefore you are not consumed, O sons of Jacob. Malachi 3:6

Further, God is a Covenant-keeper, for instance, He kept His promises with Abraham and Moses at different occasions while dealing with these two individuals, see (Genesis 17:9-11 and Exodus 3:15). There are many other instances in the Bible that show that God can keep His promises whenever and wherever, for many years, even thousands of years. Let us read,

> And God said to Abraham: "As for you, you shall keep My covenant, you and your descendants after you throughout their generations. 10 This is My covenant which you shall keep, between Me and you and your descendants after you: Every male child among you shall be circumcised; 11 and you shall be circumcised in the flesh of your foreskins, and it shall be a sign of the covenant between Me and you. Genesis 17:9-11

> Moreover God said to Moses, "Thus you shall say to the children of Israel: 'The LORD God of your fathers, the God of Abraham, the God of Isaac, and the God of Jacob, has sent me to you. This is My name forever, and this is My memorial to all generations.' Exodus 3:15

Unsurprisingly, God was interested in saving the people of Nineveh (an Assyrian capital city during the time), from damnation because of their sins. God's love for this city which was abroad led to the decision to send Jonah to them if they would repent. It had nothing to do with Jonah, Jonah's genealogical root, that is, the tribe of Zebulun, or the political animosity between the two nations—God is God of the entire universe.

For some of us, it might not come as a surprise hearing Jonah's name being mentioned for the first time through the imminent judgment on Nineveh. But it is important to mention that Jonah prophesied in Israel before the Nineveh missional assignment. It is recorded that his prediction for Israel was fulfilled during the reign of King Jeroboam II. This king, (Jeroboam II) continued with the recovery agenda which his predecessor (Jehoash) had began. Jeroboam II was a good administrator and military general who recovered all the territories Israel had lost, (2 Kings 14:28), but he broke Yahweh's covenant continually, because of idol worship,[1] despite the economic recovery which was credited to his reign.

> Now the rest of the acts of Jeroboam, and all that he did—his might, how he made war, and how he recaptured for Israel, from Damascus and Hamath, what had belonged to Judah—are they not written in the book of the chronicles of the kings of Israel? 2 Kings 14:28

In a few words, Jeroboam II was successful in his political office, but did not walk in the will of God. Pray like this,

---

1 Harold Stigers, Writing on 2 Kings in Charles F. Pfeiffer, The Wycliffe Bible Commentary, Chicago: Moody Press, 1962, p. 353

God of Israel, give me the grace to walk in your will and grant me success in my career in the name of Jesus Christ

Father, give me the power to walk in your will and grant me success in my ministry in the name of Jesus Christ

God of Israel, give me the will-power to walk in obedience and grant me success in my business in the name of Jesus Christ, amen.

As for Jonah, although his missionary duty to Nineveh (a non-Israelite city) is more popular to a lot of people today, yet this aspect of his ministry during Jeroboam II must not be overlooked. Let us read (2 Kings 14:23-25),

Meanwhile, over in Israel, Jeroboam II had become king during the fifteenth year of the reign of King Amaziah of Judah. Jeroboam's reign lasted forty-one years. 24 But he was as evil as Jeroboam I (the son of Nebat), who had led Israel into the sin of worshiping idols. 25 Jeroboam II recovered the lost territories of Israel between Hamath and the Dead Sea, just as the Lord God of Israel had predicted through Jonah (son of Amittai) the prophet from Gathhepher. 2 Kings 14:23-25 TLB

Jonah As A Human Agent

Humans by nature are vulnerable and fragile like a worm crawling in an open field, anything can happen to it. Also, humans can be timid and weak except God's mercy that regularly keeps us strong in the face of challenges or crisis. Lest we forget, Jonah was a messenger of God, but he was a human agent. However, we should be grateful for God's merciful kindness towards us as the Bible states in (Psalms 103:13-14; 136:23-24, Lamentation 3:22-23). Let us read,

> As a father pities his children, So the LORD pities those who fear Him. 14 For He knows our frame; He remembers that we are dust. Psalm 103:13-14

> (It is God) Who remembered us in our lowly state, For His mercy endures forever; 24 And rescued us from our enemies, For His mercy endures forever. Psalm 136:23-24

> Through the LORD's mercies we are not consumed, Because His compassions fail not. 23 They are new every morning; Great is Your faithfulness. Lamentation 3:22-23

How Does The Bible Describe Jonah?

The Bible describes Jonah as someone who ran away from God, (Jonah 1:3),

> But Jonah rose up to flee unto Tarshish from the presence of the LORD, and went down to Joppa; and he found a ship going to Tarshish: so he paid the fare thereof, and went down into it, to go with them unto Tarshish from the presence of the LORD. Jonah 1:3

It should be considered a serious incident for a child of God to leave God's presence the way Jonah did. Is anything wrong with having the mind of your own? Not really, but he (Jonah) was a man of God who was expected to be a good example. You and I as God's children are equally required to lead a good example at all times. It is completely strange when we consider that in God's presence there is fullness of joy and in His right hand are good and perfect things (pleasures) forever more, (Psalm 16:11), and flee His presence. Yet, Jonah fled from God's presence. The irony of life is that, any of us could have behaved in a like manner. Unfortunately there is need to ask further harder questions when Jonah behaved differently at this time.

What made the opportunity for repentance that God wanted to offer the Ninevites to mean nothing to Jonah at that time? What went wrong with Jonah's thinking ability? One of our instincts should be to enter into Jonah's world, perhaps we can learn something from his perspective. Warning! We do not have to downplay the situation and make it look simple, ordinary and normal. Not at all.

However, it must have been concerning to him because that was not his first encounter with God. The question arises, is God about to use him to teach us something, or show how weak any of us could be during a crisis of some sort? This is my opinion, any of us could be the 'Jonah' here. Would I, or yourself have behaved any better? At this time period, there are five pointers or questions which have been generated below to help you form some mental objects in your quest to obtain mercy. Be ready.

Question Time

- To start with, what could have informed Jonah's decision—personally, socio-economically and politically?
- What was his mental state at the time—angry, anxious, bitter, confused, depressed, overwhelmed, or fearful?
- What would likely be his immediate circumstance during that time, that is, family matters, financial challenges, pressure from Ministry workload, or something else?
- Were there internal conflict, or external forces, a spiritual battle, or some trouble somewhere, to have warranted the behaviour?

- Was his Ministry facing problems, or he had family related issues, or both? Perhaps we would never know.

There's Need For Discernment

But note, not everyone you see on the streets is a happy person. They could be carrying some baggage of problems. Nevertheless, this is my guess, Jonah could be wrong in our eyes and we are allowed to criticise, or conclude that he acted disobediently to God. However, as a human, I think he had his reservations. Let us be reminded that being a servant of God does not exclude one from facing crisis in their life. Have you made a mistake before? Cast the first stone and let us see.

Interestingly, as we progress in life, we are likely to have one 'Jonah' or the other in our 'ship' (life) which could lead to a misfortune. Remember, as Jonah boarded the ship going to Tarshish and got them into trouble, so people can enter your life, looking harmless and innocent at first, until after some time then the storm begins. The 'ship' in question could be through a person you have allowed into your space, someone you have given too much access into your private or personal life. For instance, an associate from your school or the university, through your church fellowship meeting, a partner in business, someone you dated, or in a courtship with a person before marriage, a lifetime relationship of any kind, and so on. This is why it is important to beware of people you allow access into your life ('ship'), intentionally or unintentionally. We all need discernment without being too suspicious of any person who comes into our lives.

Going forward, following the storm at sea, I imagine the sailors regretted that their passengers were not properly vetted before they allowed them to board the ship. Was there a situation in your life that you wished you were more cautious? The sailors would have thought so when the trouble arose. Hear my piece of advice, always try to do the right thing to avoid a regret later.

May God deliver you from dangerous people in your life, whether they look innocent now or harmless. Hear this, not long into the journey a storm arose and Jonah as we know, was responsible for the loss of their economic goods, and it almost cost the entire lives of the mariners and their fellow travellers. Again, I pray that you will not welcome or attach yourself to wrong people in the name of Jesus Christ. Always remember, your 'ship' in this context could be your business, marriage, talent, skill, ministry, career, to mention but this few.

Furthermore, as much as possible, avoid destiny destroyers or polluters, and such people who think they can do whatever they like. Note that Jonah in the above text was a dangerous passenger, but he didn't look like it when he first boarded the ship. In the previous two chapters, it could be seen that Jonah already found himself in the midst of the socio-economic and political nuances of his time. Having been caught in the web, it is pertinent to enter his world—his space, to enable us to truly know him as it would be seen in the next chapter. Let no one judge or blame him.

CHAPTER THREE
WELCOME TO JONAH'S WORLD

Jonahic Factor

One might not really appreciate the vastness of God's mercy which was shown to Jonah, unless they understand how he took things in his own hands. He had thought that he could do whatever he wanted in his own way, and in his own right. Considering the way Jonah behaved, why should a runaway prophet be spared when faced by an imminent death? Did the Bible not say that the soul that sins shall die? (Ezekiel 18:20). However, in order to understand what I call the Jonahic factor, we have to consider some possible variables, and ponder over some scenarios, such as provided below:

- Who deserves to be shown mercy at the current climate—anybody?
- Does Jonah deserve to be shown mercy the way he went about things initially, during and after the tempest? More on this later.

Nineveh—The Heathen City

Interestingly, the only prophecy contained in the Book of Jonah is about Nineveh, an Assyrian capital city which was a heathen metropolis at the time. Nineveh at that period was located at an important trade routes between the north to south, and east to west with a peculiar advantage around the tributary of River Tigris. In this present day, the ruins of Nineveh can be found in Iraq at a city called Mosul.[2]

Jonah In Another Planet?

What was the implication of Jonah being sent to Nineveh? What is the unique assignment that God can use you for, locally, and internationally? Would you have obliged Him if you were Jonah? As realised later, why should heathens be preached to, only once and they repented, but Israel who boasted as being God's elect refused on several occasions to heed God's warnings? Additionally, why was it difficult for Jonah to accept an instant instruction, despite God's direction for him to go to Nineveh? If Jonah wanted to "mind his own business" as it were, does that mean he should respond as if to say, "nobody should order me around?" Definitely, it appears Jonah was living in another planet.

God's Expectation, Can We Know It?

Further, what could have been on God's mind while sending Jonah to the city of this sworn adversary of Israel during that time—love, compassion, judgment, forgiveness, or nothing? Regardless, God had some expectations from both Jonah and the Ninevites he was sent to. Even so, it is paramount to remember that people can go to any length to justify their actions, often-times like Jonah tried to do. Lest I forget, human beings can intentionally decide to retain, omit, or delete some facts to suit their intentions and purposes in order to achieve their goals which could be questionable and selfish which should not be strange to us.

As we consider the nature of Jonah's behaviour, either that at a stage in our lives we were like 'Jonah' who needed to

---

2 www.britannica.com/place/Nineveh. Cited on 12 /07/2024

repent and walk in obedience, or behaved like one of the people in 'Nineveh' that God's heart is yearning after to repent, and thus be saved from judgment and destruction which were imminent. Whichever way one thinks, God has genuine intention behind whatever He does, as such, it could be that He wanted to use this Nineveh case as a reproof to Israel who despite having prophets with them at all times, failed to obey the warnings of Yahweh.[3]

If Jonah as a prophet went the opposite direction when he was sent on this missional assignment, what should be expected from the people they were supposed to guide? Would the people of Nineveh that Jonah was sent to, behave any better or repent? How many of us are ready to behave better and please God from today? Let us read (Jonah 3:4-10),

> And Jonah began to enter the city on the first day's walk. Then he cried out and said, "Yet forty days, and Nineveh shall be overthrown!" 5 So the people of Nineveh believed God, proclaimed a fast, and put on sackcloth, from the greatest to the least of them. 6 Then word came to the king of Nineveh; and he arose from his throne and laid aside his robe, covered himself with sackcloth and sat in ashes. 7 And he caused it to be proclaimed and published throughout Nineveh by the decree of the king and his nobles, saying, Let neither man nor beast, herd nor flock, taste anything; do not let them eat, or drink water.

> 8 But let man and beast be covered with sackcloth, and cry mightily to God; yes, let every one turn from his evil way and from the violence that is in his hands.

---

3   Jamieson, Fausset and Brown, Commentary On the Whole Bible, Grand Rapids, Michigan: Zondervan Publishing House, 1961, p. 805

9 Who can tell if God will turn and relent, and turn away from His fierce anger, so that we may not perish? 10 Then God saw their works, that they turned from their evil way; and God relented from the disaster that He had said He would bring upon them, and He did not do it. Jonah 3:4-10

An Unexpected Turnaround

What an incredible turn of event! Humans and beasts at Nineveh fasted, repented and submitted obediently to God, and He rescinded His judgment true to His word (Jeremiah 18:4-8),

> And the vessel that he made of clay was marred in the hand of the potter; so he made it again into another vessel, as it seemed good to the potter to make. 5 Then the word of the LORD came to me, saying: 6 "O house of Israel, can I not do with you as this potter?" says the LORD. "Look, as the clay is in the potter's hand, so are you in My hand, O house of Israel! 7 The instant I speak concerning a nation and concerning a kingdom, to pluck up, to pull down, and to destroy it, 8 if that nation against whom I have spoken turns from its evil, I will relent of the disaster that I thought to bring upon it. Jeremiah 18:4-8

But Jonah was unhappy when he saw that they (the Ninevites) had repented and were pardoned by God. Why should that be his response? Most likely, because of his ego and inborn hatred for the Assyrians. If God was requiring you to do something and it was done, to whose glory it should be? Is it right to be angry because people obeyed God? It seems to me that we are seeing the authentic human side of Jonah we never knew, and essentially, this is a reflection of a part of our lives too. Nobody is perfect, but this Jonahic behaviour must stop. May you see Jonah's human side and correct yourself.

Way forward, should God be merciful to you, would you like Him to be merciful to other people or not? Would it be appropriate to reciprocate God's mercy in people's life or not? In my opinion, we all should be doing that. Jonah's story makes an interesting reading in that he attracted a terrible storm into the ship which could ideally be likened to someone's life, business, ministry or home. However, God intervened, showed mercy, and saved his life and the others (the mariners and their co-travellers), but he (Jonah) would not like God to save others. What an irony of life!

Prayer Points

Any person attracting storm into my life and business, fail completely from this moment in the name of Jesus Christ— fail now and forever in the name of Jesus Christ

Any personality attracting storm into my ministry and home, fail totally in your wicked agenda in the name of Jesus Christ—fail totally in the name of Jesus Christ

Any syndicate attracting any type of storm into my career and destiny, fail woefully in your evil mission in the name of Jesus Christ—fail woefully in the name of Jesus Christ

Every contrary wind attracted by known forces or my relations, disappear from my life from today in the name of Jesus Christ

Every satanic wind attracted by unknown forces, disappear from my life from today in the name of Jesus Christ

Every contrary wind operating through my bloodline, disappear from my life from today in the name of Jesus Christ, amen.

Jonah's appearance at a stage meant negative and looked like a corrupt personality on board the ship, pray like this: Every negative and corrupt personality working against my life, be destroyed completely from now in the name of Jesus Christ

Every situation that is presenting me in a negative way, reverse by fire, in the name of Jesus Christ

Every negative and corrupt agent working against my divine assignment, be destroyed totally from now in the name of Jesus Christ

Every negative and corrupt agent working against my divine opportunities, be terminated totally from now in the name of Jesus Christ

Every negative and corrupt agent working against my talent and skill, be destroyed totally from now in the name of Jesus Christ

Every negative and corrupt personality working against my blessings and ordained goals in my life, be destroyed completely from now in the name of Jesus Christ, amen.

Jonah And The Debtor in (Matthew 18:23-34)

Therefore the kingdom of heaven is like a certain king who wanted to settle accounts with his servants. 24 And when he had begun to settle accounts, one was brought to him who owed him ten thousand talents.

25 But as he was not able to pay, his master commanded that he be sold, with his wife and children and all that he had, and that payment be made. 26 The servant therefore fell down before him, saying, 'Master, have patience with me, and I will pay you all.' 27 Then the master of that servant was moved with compassion, released him, and forgave him the debt. 28 "But that servant went out and found one of his fellow servants who owed him a hundred denarii; and he laid hands on him and took him by the throat, saying, 'Pay me what you owe!' 29 So his fellow servant fell down at his feet and begged him, saying, 'Have patience with me, and I will pay you all.' 30 And he would not, but went and threw him into prison till he should pay the debt. 31 So when his fellow servants saw what had been done, they were very grieved, and came and told their master all that had been done. 32 Then his master, after he had called him, said to him, 'You wicked servant! I forgave you all that debt because you begged me. 33 Should you not also have had compassion on your fellow servant, just as I had pity on you?' 34 And his master was angry, and delivered him to the torturers until he should pay all that was due to him. Matthew 18:23-34

Could it be that Jonah was a mean individual, insensitive, selfish, self-centred, or an ingrate? What does Jonah really want? He was like as narrated above, a servant who was forgiven so much, but didn't want to forgive the other person their little debts. It is about time we learn properly from this runaway evangelist.

A Plant, Or Human Lives, Which Should Matter?

The difference between Jonah and the servant referred to above (Matthew 18:23-34) is that, the latter was punished forthwith and heavily, because he was not exemplary and compassionate. However, for Jonah, it was a different method that God applied. Have you observed if God is using a particular way to handle your case? I suggest you reflect deeply and comprehensively before you jump to conclusion. As we can see, God took Jonah through a different experience by using a plant which caught the latter's attention.

The plan was, God made the plant to grow and it provided a shade for Jonah then God caused it to be eaten up by worms so that Jonah could learn through the scotching heat of the day (Jonah 4:5-11). Before we move on, are you, or someone you know is going through "a scotching heat" experience? I ask God for mercy for such ones and may the circumstance turnaround for the better in the name of Jesus Christ. Let us read,

> So Jonah went out of the city and sat on the east side of the city. There he made himself a shelter and sat under it in the shade, till he might see what would become of the city. 6 And the LORD God prepared a plant and made it come up over Jonah, that it might be shade for his head to deliver him from his misery. So Jonah was very grateful for the plant. 7 But as morning dawned the next day God prepared a worm, and it so damaged the plant that it withered. 8 And it happened, when the sun arose, that God prepared a vehement east wind; and the sun beat on Jonah's head, so that he grew faint. Then he wished death for himself, and said, "It is better for me to die than to live." 9 Then God said to Jonah, "Is it right for you to be angry about the plant?" And he said, "It is right for me to be angry, even to death!" 10 But the LORD said, "You have had pity on the plant for which you

have not labored, nor made it grow, which came up in a night and perished in a night. 11 And should I not pity Nineveh, that great city, in which are more than one hundred and twenty thousand persons who cannot discern between their right hand and their left—and much livestock?" Jonah 4:5-11

It is possible Jonah had a changed attitude after the practical attendance of this "Plant" tutorial class that was given to him by God. If so, it should be deemed as mercy which came out of God's kindness or grace (*chesed*). It is amazing that God considered it fit to pardon the prophet who didn't deserve it. It is hoped that henceforth, Jonah would become humble and compassionate towards people. I encourage all my readers to cherish this moral excellence, be humble and compassionate to people.

Prayer Points

Lord God of Israel—from today give me the grace to walk in obedience in my entire life in the name of Jesus Christ

Father of mercy and compassion, from now give me the grace to do your will all the days of my life in the name of Jesus Christ

Lord God of Israel—henceforth, give me the grace to be a worthy ambassador of your kingdom throughout my lifetime in the name of Jesus Christ, amen.

Does God Expect You To Be Merciful?

Should God be merciful to you, would you like Him to be merciful to other people or not? Undoubtedly, God is full of compassion and mercy already, it is left for us to ask Him for it, (Psalm 86:15-17) reads,

> But You, O Lord, *are* a God full of compassion, and gracious, Longsuffering and abundant in mercy and truth. 16 Oh, turn to me, and have mercy on me! Give Your strength to Your servant, And save the son of Your maidservant. 17 Show me a sign for good, That those who hate me may see it and be ashamed, Because You, LORD, have helped me and comforted me. Psalm 86:15-17

Also read (Jeremiah 30:18),

> "Thus says the LORD: 'Behold, I will bring back the captivity of Jacob's tents, And have mercy on his dwelling places; The city shall be built upon its own mound, And the palace shall remain according to its own plan. Jeremiah 30:18

Additionally, God's heart yearns after His children because of His mercy, (Jeremiah 31:20) reads:

> Is Ephraim My dear son? Is he a pleasant child? For though I spoke against him, I earnestly remember him still; Therefore My heart yearns for him; I will surely have mercy on him, says the LORD. Jeremiah 31:20

There are consequences for those who fail to show mercy, candidly they can get into God's trouble as it happened to an individual sometime ago in the Bible, (Daniel 4:27).

> Therefore, O king, let my advice be acceptable to you; break off your sins by being righteous, and

your iniquities by showing mercy to the poor. Perhaps there may be a lengthening of your prosperity." Daniel 4:27

Does God expect you to be merciful? Yes. Therefore, it is not surprising when Jonah himself advises us to not throw away mercy, (Jonah 2:8),

Those who regard worthless idols Forsake their own Mercy. Jonah 2:8

A Special Tip—if you ever think God is angry with you, cry out for His mercy and He will relent, (Habakkuk 3:2).

O LORD, I have heard Your speech and was afraid; O LORD, revive Your work in the midst of the years! In the midst of the years make it known; In wrath remember mercy. Habakkuk 3:2

Take Heed! It is a serious matter—never take God for granted. Once upon a time He was angry with the people of Israel for seventy years, but when His prophet pleaded on behalf of the people, God returned to them because of His mercy, mercy is powerful (Zechariah 1:12-16).

Then the Angel of the LORD answered and said, "O LORD of hosts, how long will You not have mercy on Jerusalem and on the cities of Judah, against which You were angry these seventy years?" 13 And the LORD answered the angel who talked to me, with good and comforting words. 14 So the angel who spoke with me said to me, , "Proclaim, saying, 'Thus says the LORD of hosts: I am zealous for Jerusalem And for Zion with great zeal. 15 I am exceedingly angry with the nations at ease; For I was a

little angry, And they helped—but with evil intent."
16 'Therefore thus says the LORD: I am returning to
Jerusalem with mercy; My house shall be built in it," says
the LORD of hosts, "And a surveyor's line shall be stretched
out over Jerusalem." ' Zechariah 1:12-16

God encourages that mercy be duplicated and be shown to
our fellows. It is not good to enjoy God's mercies alone,
only selfish and wicked people do that, (Zechariah 7:9) says,

"Thus says the LORD of hosts: 'Execute true justice,
Show mercy and compassion Everyone to his brother.
Zechariah 7:9

Also, note that blessed are the merciful, for they shall obtain
mercy, (Matthew 5:7). Always remember that because of
mercy God can start afresh with you and treat you as if you
never wronged, or sinned against Him. Many times and at
different occasion the Israelites would disobey God, but
after leaving them for some time, God hears their plea
because of His *chesed* (kindness + grace). In other words,
His mercy) as we read in (Zechariah 10:6).

I will strengthen the house of Judah, And I will save the
house of Joseph. I will bring them back, Because I have
mercy on them. They shall be as though I had not cast
them aside; For I am the LORD their God, And I will
hear them. Zechariah 10:6

Learn Good Example From Others

Before this time, Jesus had healed a woman who was
haemorrhaging for twelve years, this happened while He
was going to raise a dead girl who was the daughter of one
of the rulers as narrated in (Matthew 9:18-26). It was a busy

THE UNIVERSALITY OF GOD'S MERCIES: THE BOOK OF JONAH

schedule, but Jesus had time for each of them. Whenever you need God's help, He will attend to you. Remember, this book is about the mercies of God, therefore, learn from the two blind men who cried for mercy when Jesus was passing around their neighbourhood on a particular day, see (Matthew 9:27-30). Ask for mercy right now, and may God have mercy on you from today.

> When Jesus departed from there, two blind men followed Him, crying out and saying, "Son of David, have mercy on us!" 28 And when He had come into the house, the blind men came to Him. And Jesus said to them, "Do you believe that I am able to do this?" They said to Him, "Yes, Lord." 29 Then He touched their eyes, saying, "According to your faith let it be to you." 30 And their eyes were opened. And Jesus sternly warned them, saying, "See that no one knows it." Matthew 9:27-30. More discussions are available in Chapter Thirteen of this book.

God expects us to be merciful to people, be sensitive and respond accordingly. As depicted above, God exemplifies mercy in many instances, hence my resolve that, it is not good to enjoy God's mercies alone, only selfish and wicked people do that. Note that, we are commanded to "show mercy and compassion, everyone to his brother," (Zechariah 7:9). If you thought that the behaviour of the evangelist who took things in his own hands initially was acceptable, and by that should not face outright judgment, the uniqueness of Jonah's commission in the next chapter might shed some light for a change of heart. For the critical minds, let me ask, considering the way Jonah behaved, why did God spared the life of the runaway prophet when faced by an imminent death? Did the Bible (Ezekiel 18:20), not say that the soul who sins shall die?

The soul who sins shall die. The son shall not bear the guilt of the father, nor the father bear the guilt of the son. The righteousness of the righteous shall be upon himself, and the wickedness of the wicked shall be upon himself. Ezekiel 18:20

The Lord has spoken.

CHAPTER FOUR
THE UNIQUENESS OF JONAH'S COMMISSION

No More Excuses

To start the journey into Jonah's commission which is unique in many ways, imagine a world where the Managing Director (MD) of an organisation instructs his staff to do some work for him, but the staff blatantly refused and left for a vacation to a different city. Imagine the situation from the simplest uncomplicated point of view. One can say that the individual would lose his or her job, because the person has undermined the authority, or their superior. Let us assume this person to be Jonah, and God as the MD. Impliedly, it could have meant that Jonah was disrespectful to his MD, irresponsible, not a good team player, resentful, arrogant, and unsuitable to work in that establishment, and so on. In which ever way this example is considered, there can be excuses for why the staff went on a vacation, for instance, by saying that mental and psychological issues happened to him (Jonah). Regardless, Jonah might have caused more harm than good to a lot of people in the office. Of course, he erred against the All-knowing God, and it is dangerous to disobey the One who can give and take life. No excuses, God sees and knows about everything.

God Is Slow To Anger But Abundant In Mercy

In contrast, one can make excuses for Jonah by saying, for example, he was probably planning for a journey of self-discovery when God sent him, or it was meant to be a personal journey for his self-realisation. But to be honest, even where there was a struggle, or a turmoil in Jonah's life at that time, it was possible for God to heal him, or not send him on the missional task at all. The fact remains that, Jonah refused to go to Nineveh the first time he was instructed by God to go there. Realistically, Jonah the servant of God, had thought that the Ninevites did not deserve to be warned that God would destroy them within forty days unless they repented from their wickedness.

The evangelist had forgotten that nobody can exhaust God's patience, He (God) is merciful, gracious and slow to anger, but abounds in mercy, (Psalm 103:8). Being the case, whether Jonah was adamant or not, God repeated the instruction the second time before Jonah took God seriously, (Jonah 3:1-4). Should such individual be shown mercy? We shall soon find out. Let us read,

> Now the word of the LORD came to Jonah the second time, saying, 2 "Arise, go to Nineveh, that great city, and preach to it the message that I tell you." 3 So Jonah arose and went to Nineveh, according to the word of the LORD. Now Nineveh was an exceedingly great city, a three-day journey in extent. 4 And Jonah began to enter the city on the first day's walk. Then he cried out and said, "Yet forty days, and Nineveh shall be overthrown!" Jonah 3:1-4

On a personal note, should people wait till they are threatened with storm, sickness, death, or get punished before they behave well? I do not think so. But who were the parties involved here? We are talking about God on the one hand, Jonah the evangelist as the in-between person, and the Ninevites—a population of one hundred and twenty thousand people whose lives were in danger. Unfortunately, it wasn't as straightforward as one might be thinking now. It was an interconnected case because any decision would cause a ripple effect in the other sections of the community, see Figure 1.

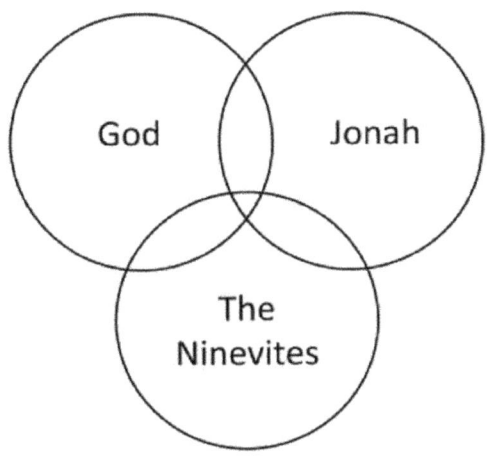

Figure 1

Response To Figure 1

The imminent danger or judgment God intended for the Ninevites did not bother Jonah, the servant of God at that time. Humanly speaking, an individual like Jonah should not be shown mercy at this point, because he was not ready to show mercy to others. Is it possible for God who is full of mercy to refuse to have mercy on Jonah? If not much, should God go ahead and show Jonah a little bit of mercy? Furthermore, should God proceed, what would you call this type of mercy? What makes any person feel that the Ninevites do not deserve mercy?

One wonders what was really wrong with Jonah—can any individual be bigger than God? Why should Jonah play

God? It is unfortunate but true that, sometimes we have some people like this prophet in our lives, at our workplaces, in society and our churches.

What to do?

Before we rush to cite Bible passages, when people are temperamental or lost in their own world (at some point in life like Jonah), we need to be sensitive in handling their condition because they might need some medical help apart from the spiritual, and they must not be denied the opportunity. Further, there is need for discernment, because the condition can be manipulated by the devil. We need to pray for such individuals, and practically be involved in their lives, for example, by accompanying them on their appointments, or be there for a visit as a friend. Additionally, show them love, and do everything in love, as expressed in (1 Corinthians 16:14).

> Let all that you do be done with love. 1 Corinthians 16:14

However, there is need to maintain helpful and necessary disciplinary or corrective measures, where and when required. For some people in our churches, there's need for patience because sometimes it could appear harsh, or hurtful when rehabilitation is going on, but afterwards, the end result would benefit the individual and the body of Christ, as stated in (Hebrews 12:11). Let us read,

> Now no chastening seems to be joyful for the present, but painful; nevertheless, afterward it yields the peaceable fruit of righteousness to those who have been trained by it. Hebrews 12:11

God Is Not Your Mate, Learn From Abraham

Overall, as God's children we need to tread carefully because God is not our equal or mate. Can the clay say to the potter you lack understanding, or I will show you how you should mould me? Never! Let us read (Jeremiah 29:16),

> Surely you have things turned around! Shall the potter be esteemed as the clay; For shall the thing made say of him who made it, "He did not make me"? Or shall the thing formed say of him who formed it, "He has no understanding"? Jeremiah 29:16

It seems Jonah wanted to do things in his own way. Far be it, that a mere mortal would dictate to the One who is called the Almighty God. Let us remember what Abraham did at the place of intercession before the destruction of Sodom and Gomorrah took place. He (Abraham) was a friend of God, (James 2:23b), but never behaved like Jonah. The patriarch (Abraham) never overstepped his boundary, never dictated to God, and never tried to do things in his own way. What the patriarch did during the intercession was remarkable and is worth emulating. Concisely, he approached God with reverence, humility, and faith, to name but a few. In spite of Abraham's privileged position, he never behaved as if God was his mate, this can be confirmed in (Genesis 18:20-33) which reads,

> And the LORD said, "Because the outcry against Sodom and Gomorrah is great, and because their sin is very grave, 21 I will go down now and see whether they have done altogether according to the outcry against it that has come to Me; and if not, I will know." 22 Then the men turned away from there and went toward Sodom, but Abraham still stood before the LORD. 23 And Abraham came near and said, "Would You also destroy

the righteous with the wicked? 24 Suppose there were fifty righteous within the city; would You also destroy the place and not spare it for the fifty righteous that were in it? 25 Far be it from You to do such a thing as this, to slay the righteous with the wicked, so that the righteous should be as the wicked; far be it from You! Shall not the Judge of all the earth do right?"

26 So the LORD said, "If I find in Sodom fifty righteous within the city, then I will spare all the place for their sakes." 27 Then Abraham answered and said, "Indeed now, I who am but dust and ashes have taken it upon myself to speak to the Lord: 28 Suppose there were five less than the fifty righteous; would You destroy all of the city for lack of five?" So He said, "If I find there forty-five, I will not destroy it." 29 And he spoke to Him yet again and said, "Suppose there should be forty found there?" So He said, "I will not do it for the sake of forty."

30 Then he said, "Let not the Lord be angry, and I will speak: Suppose thirty should be found there?" So He said, "I will not do it if I find thirty there." 31 And he said, "Indeed now, I have taken it upon myself to speak to the Lord: Suppose twenty should be found there?" So He said, "I will not destroy it for the sake of twenty." 32 Then he said, "Let not the Lord be angry, and I will speak but once more: Suppose ten should be found there?" And He said, "I will not destroy it for the sake of ten." 33 So the LORD went His way as soon as He had finished speaking with Abraham; and Abraham returned to his place. Genesis 18:20-33

We Can Learn From The Patriarch (Abraham)

Were it possible, Jonah should have been recommended to go and learn from the patriarch (Abraham) about how to talk to

God. Having been privileged to talk with God, Abraham shows us that, intercession requires empathy, tactfulness, wisdom, veneration and deep respect for God. We can apply all these pillars in our daily worship and dealings with God. Caution! It is dangerous to engage in a wilful misbehaviour like Jonah did when he was given God's commission to go and warn the Assyrians, but he decided to go somewhere else, as presented in (Jonah 1:2-3) which reads,

> Arise, go to Nineveh, that great city, and cry out against it; for their wickedness has come up before Me." 3 But Jonah arose to flee to Tarshish from the presence of the LORD. He went down to Joppa, and found a ship going to Tarshish; so he paid the fare, and went down into it, to go with them to Tarshish from the presence of the LORD. Jonah 1:2-3

The Place Of Mercy

In any case, we are faced with some variables at this stage. Let us start by asking: should a runaway prophet remain in God's good books? Not only a runaway evangelist, but he also failed to be empathetic. How possible is it for someone with national hatred for the Assyrians, ingrained anger, and bitterness come before the Lord? I mean, Holy God, Righteous God, the True Judge of the whole earth? It is evidently clear that during that time, the evangelist's heart was not pure and was in contrary to the scripture, (Psalm 24:3-4a). How do you reconcile this situation, humanly speaking?

> Who may ascend into the hill of the LORD? Or who may stand in His holy place? 4 He who has clean hands and a pure heart. Psalm 24:3-4a

Apparently, Jonah had disqualified himself before God, but mercy which originated from God's kindness or grace (*chesed*) answered for him and he was spared. I pray for God's mercy to qualify you where you supposed to be disqualified, and let mercy prevail in all your cases in the name of Jesus Christ. I pray for you: no matter how terrible your case, mercy will prevail over judgment for you in the name of Jesus Christ, amen.

Furthermore, let God's kindness be your portion in the name of Jesus Christ of Nazareth. Considering God's mercy that sprang out of His grace or kindness (*chesed)* for Jonah, but '*charis*' as used in the New Testament also implies grace. My question: what should be one's response to the New Testament '*charis*' which somehow implies grace? Simply, we should receive such grace with both hands and of a truth, we all need grace.

Where The Two Meet—Chesed Versus Charis

The fact about *chesed* (meaning kindness or grace), as seen in the Old Testament (OT) is that, the 'grace' compelled God to journey with His people by granting them hope and purpose. For now, that grace is partially similar to *charis* in the New Testament (NT), as in Figure 2, 'grace' is a common denominator here.

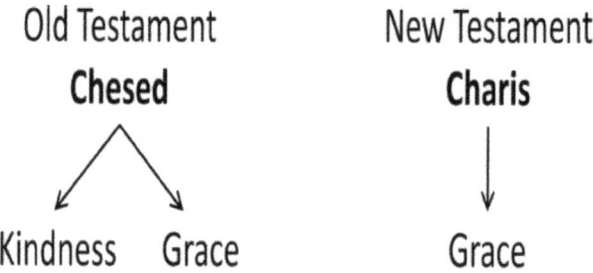

Figure 2

But in Figure 3 below, there is a twist. As presented below in Figure 3, they (*chesed* and *charis*) are not completely the same. You have kindness or grace (chesed) in the OT, whereas, you have *charis* (meaning grace) in the NT, see figure 2 above.

But to expatiate further, the word 'grace' in regards to the NT section above, (referring to *charis*), includes God's concern for man in his guilt, and also God's concern for man in his despair,[4] see Figure 3.

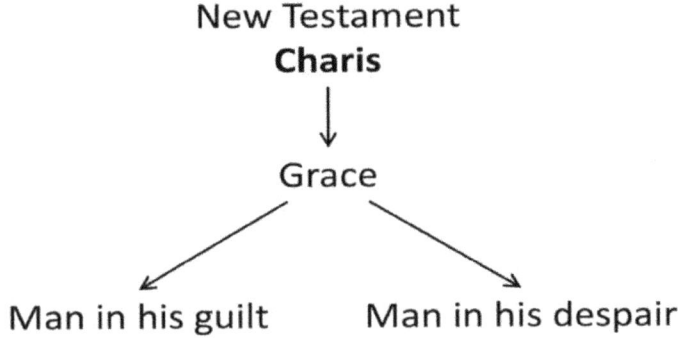

New Testament
Charis

Grace

Man in his guilt   Man in his despair

Figure 3

Firstly, let us consider *charis as* God's concern for human in his guilt, (including male and female persons), for all have sinned, (Romans 3:22-24). Let us read,

> Even the righteousness of God, through faith in Jesus Christ, to all and on all who believe. For there is no difference; 23 for all have sinned and fall short of the glory of God, 24 being justified freely by His grace through the redemption that is in Christ Jesus. Romans 3:22-24

---

4 Derek Williams, (Ed.,), New Concise Bible Dictionary, Leicester, England: Inter-Varsity Press, 1989, p. 347

Typically, the Adamic sin in (Genesis 3) was concerning. Of course, God had to come up with His Redemption Plan later. Briefly, in regards to redemption in the NT, it required Christ, the Son of God to die on the Cross for the salvation of the souls of humankind. It was a costly process which involved Christ's precious blood, (1 Peter 1:18-19),

> Knowing that you were not redeemed with corruptible things, like silver or gold, from your aimless conduct received by tradition from your fathers, 19 but with the precious blood of Christ, as of a lamb without blemish and without spot. 1 Peter 1:18-19

Example of Man In His Guilt

However, there is the sin which as humans we face in our daily lives which inevitably without God's help, we would be condemned on the spot. Undoubtedly, there are failings which are regular or daily in nature, which make people compromise, lie, angry, steal, commit sexual immorality, to mention but a few. One of such challenges which was brought to Jesus Christ was clearly presented in (John 8:3-11). Let us read,

> Then the scribes and Pharisees brought to Him a woman caught in adultery. And when they had set her in the midst, 4 they said to Him, "Teacher, this woman was caught in adultery, in the very act. 5 Now Moses, in the law, commanded us that such should be stoned. But what do You say?" 6 This they said, testing Him, that they might have something of which to accuse Him. But Jesus stooped down and wrote on the ground with His finger, as though He did not hear.

7 So when they continued asking Him, He raised Himself up and said to them, "He who is without sin among you, let him throw a stone at her first." 8 And again He stooped down and wrote on the ground. 9 Then those who heard it, being convicted by their conscience, went out one by one, beginning with the oldest even to the last. And Jesus was left alone, and the woman standing in the midst. 10 When Jesus had raised Himself up and saw no one but the woman, He said to her, "Woman, where are those accusers [i]of yours? Has no one condemned you?" 11 She said, "No one, Lord." And Jesus said to her, "Neither do I condemn you; go and sin no more." John 8:3-11

As presented above, a woman was caught committing an adulterous act and was brought to Jesus. But, it was a ploy to set Jesus on a direct collision with the authorities, although the Old Testament approves of such allegations for judgment (of stoning to death), to be served. Amazingly, Jesus already knew the intention of the scribes and the Pharisees. In the end, the accusers dispersed in shame and disgrace due to Jesus' non-verbal response, and the woman was forgiven. Nevertheless, she was warned that she should not sin again. Thus Jesus showed concern for the woman while she was guilty.

May God turn-away all your accusers for you. Clearly, Jesus did not endorse nor encouraged what happened, but pardoned her as a result of grace (*charis*). My conclusion in the above story is that, Jesus demonstrated His concern about human guilt.

In light of the above example, it is possible to visualise Jonah as being brought before God, and in his helpless state without any word of defence or alibi, but like that woman caught in the adulterous act was pardoned. On a general note, God is ready to forgive any sinner who comes to Him genuinely repentant of their sins—though their sins be as red as scarlet, they shall become as white as snow, (Isaiah 1:18) reads,

"Come now, and let us reason together," Says the LORD, "Though your sins are like scarlet, They shall be as white as snow; Though they are red like crimson, They shall be as wool. Isaiah 1:18

Seek Help

But more than in the above story, especially in the present fast-paced world, a world of Artificial Intelligence (AI), climate change, advanced technological softwares which are mind-blowing, and many other supersonic inventions, and other happenings both in the military, socio-economic, political and secular world generally. In spite of all the foregoing, it is possible to harbour all kinds of guilt, key among them are personal guilt, such as, murder, abortion, divorce, and feeling let down because one didn't do enough to help, financial debts, addiction to drugs, or substance abuse, loss of employment, and so on. May God have mercy on us.

All the aforementioned, can constitute a lot of pain and guilt which if help is not sought quickly, could get out of hand. They are harsh realities of life which one must admit is real, but wrong to keep any of them to oneself. What to do? Seek help in your local Church if facilities are available, confide in a trusted person, or a mature Christian believer, and let them know how you feel, and depending on how serious the matter is, get an appropriate counsellor and professional help for the type of guilt. Once again, seek help.

Majorly, I intend to limit my presentation on theological guilt, therefore, in the above provided scripture, (Isaiah 1:18), we are encouraged that, we can receive help from Jesus Christ who died for our sin, resurrected on the third day, ascended into heaven and He is coming back again to judge the world. He is always genuinely concerned about human's guilt, and will help you considering the way the woman who was allegedly caught in an adulterous act was helped—He is our Advocate and Mediator, (1 John 2 :1-2; 1 Timothy 2:3-6),

> My little children, these things I write to you, so that you may not sin. And if anyone sins, we have an Advocate with the Father, Jesus Christ the righteous. 2 And He Himself is the propitiation for our sins, and not for ours only but also for the whole world. 1 John 2:1-2

> For this is good and acceptable in the sight of God our Savior, 4 who desires all men to be saved and to come to the knowledge of the truth. 5 For there is one God and one Mediator between God and men, the Man Christ Jesus, 6 who gave Himself a ransom for all, to be testified in due time. 1 Timothy 2:3-6

No Lowering Of Standards

In agreement with how an eminent scholar astutely concluded, Jesus never relaxed His standards when He talked with the woman caught in adultery, and at no point in life would God whose standards are perfect, wink at sin, or settle for imperfection. But He forgives us unconditionally when we confess our sins.[5]

Three Examples of Man In His Despair

If *charis* also implies God's concern for man in his despair, some individuals out of many biblical examples that show God's concern for mankind in their despair, should be considered. The following three individuals without doubt showed their despair and Jesus attended to every single situation, namely, the man at the Pool of Bethesda, Jairus, and Bartimaeus.

The Desperation At Bethesda's Pool

For a start, reference can be made to where Jesus walked to the man at the Pool of Bethesda on a Sabbath day and healed him for he had been in that condition for thirty eight years, (John 5:5-9).

> Now a certain man was there who had an infirmity thirty-eight years. 6 When Jesus saw him lying there, and knew that he already had been in that condition a long time, He said to him, "Do you want to be made well?" 7 The sick man answered Him, "Sir, I have no man to put me into the pool when the water is stirred up; but while I am coming, another steps down before me." 8 Jesus said to him, "Rise, take up your bed and walk." 9 And immediately the man was made well, took up his bed, and walked. And that day was the Sabbath. John 5:5-9

---

5 Gary R. Collins, Christian Counselling: A Comprehensive Guide, Revised Edition, London: Word Publishing, 1988, p. 146

It is surprising, but spiritually possible for someone to miss opportunities that can bless their lives for many years. But extending to thirty eight years, definitely something is wrong. Notwithstanding, one day Jesus appeared unexpectedly and asked the man, "Do you want to be made well?" Don't get it wrong, the question which was asked by Jesus was a loving and compassion-filled one, but some people might not see it that way. Indeed, it was a question from a Compassionate God. Certainly, he (the man suffering the infirmity) never expected help at the time when the Man of Galilee came to him.[6]

Prayer Points

Thou Healer of the man at the Pool of Bethesda, heal me now!

Thou Healer of the man at the Pool of Bethesda, deliver me now!

Thou Healer of the man at the Pool of Bethesda, save me now!

Thou Healer of the man at the Pool of Bethesda, help me now!

Thou Healer of the man at the Pool of Bethesda, saturate my entire life with your power now! in the name of Jesus Christ

The Great Physician, touch my life emotionally, mentally and physically from today, and never allow my life to remain the same

---

6   Isaac Ajibolorunrin, Prayer Rain: An Essential Master-key for Christian Pilgrims for Retreat & The Holy Land, London: Grosvenor House Publishing Limited, 2023, pp. 89-90

Lord Jesus, touch my life medically, maritally, and vocationally in Your precious name

Exceptional solution from the Lord! locate me and deliver me from all the problems in my life in the name of Jesus Christ of Nazareth

Exceptional solution from the Lord! heal and fill up the vacuum in my life in the name of Jesus Christ of Nazareth

Exceptional solution from the Lord! deliver me from all the challenges in my life in the name of Jesus Christ of Nazareth

O Lord! single me out of the 'multitudes' and grant me miracles in the name of Jesus Christ, amen.

Please read and say the prayers that follow:

> "So I will restore to you the years that the swarming locust has eaten, The crawling locust, The consuming locust, And the chewing locust, My great army which I sent among you. 26 You shall eat in plenty and be satisfied, And praise the name of the LORD your God, Who has dealt wondrously with you; And My people shall never be put to shame. Joel 2:25-26

My Father! Compensate me for all my lost years—spiritually, financially and materially in the name of Jesus Christ of Nazareth

My Father! Compensate me for all my lost and wasted years in Ministry, let me eat in plenty and be satisfied, in the name of Jesus Christ

My Father! Compensate me for all my lost and wasted years in business, let me eat in plenty and be satisfied, in the name of Jesus Christ

Faithful Father, let all my lost and wasted years be reversed and be favourable to me from today, in the name of Jesus Christ

Almighty God, to whom nothing is impossible! Let all my lost and wasted years be reversed from today in the name of Jesus Christ

Almighty God, to whom nothing is impossible! Let all my lost and wasted years be rewarded from today in the name of Jesus Christ

Almighty God, to whom nothing is impossible! Let all my lost and wasted years be compensated for, from today in the name of Jesus Christ

Almighty Father, let all my lost and wasted years be rewarded to my advantage from today in the name of Jesus Christ

Father, treat my case with the uniqueness it requires, right now, in the name of Jesus Christ

Father, treat my case with the singularity it requires, and don't let my life remain the same again, from now in the name of Jesus Christ, amen!

The Desperation At Jairus' Home

In another instance, Jairus daughter was in a death-threatening condition, and the state of despair was very high indeed.

As recorded, while Jairus was imploring Jesus to come and heal his daughter, a message was received, stating the daughter had died, (Luke 8:41-42). What a tragedy! While the mourners were crying at home, Jesus who was delayed due to some other ecclesiastic intervention on the way, eventually arrived at the family home and raised the daughter of Jairus, (Luke 8:49-55). The end of your story shall be sweet in the name of Jesus Christ. Your story shall end well.

> And behold, there came a man named Jairus, and he was a ruler of the synagogue. And he fell down at Jesus' feet and begged Him to come to his house, 42 for he had an only daughter about twelve years of age, and she was dying … 49 While He was still speaking, someone came from the ruler of the synagogue's house, saying to him, "Your daughter is dead. Do not trouble the Teacher." 50 But when Jesus heard it, He answered him, saying, "Do not be afraid; only believe, and she will be made well." 51 When He came into the house, He permitted no one to go in except Peter, James, and John, and the father and mother of the girl. 52 Now all wept and mourned for her; but He said, "Do not weep; she is not dead, but sleeping." 53 And they ridiculed Him, knowing that she was dead. 54 But He put them all outside, took her by the hand and called, saying, "Little girl, arise." 55 Then her spirit returned, and she arose immediately. And He commanded that she be given something to eat. Luke 8:41-42, 49-55

As it turned out, the state of despair at Jairus' home disappeared because there was a type of grace (*charis*) available, and Jesus saved Jairus and his family from pain, ridicule, loss, bereavement and sorrow. The Lord will arrive on time for your situation to be resolved, and every desperation in your life will turn to celebration. Your case shall not be declared as 'too late' to receive a solution in the name of Jesus Christ.

Prayer Points

Jehovah Rapha! From today, heal every sickness in my body and in my family in the name of Jesus Christ

My Father! Turn every mourning in my life to dancing, cause celebration to manifest in my life, and let all sadness and sorrow terminate immediately, in the name of Jesus Christ

My Father! Turn every loss in my life to gain, cause shame to turn to glory and testimony in my life, and let me forget all my past sorrows from this day forward, in the name of Jesus Christ

O Lord, grant me unexpected miracles like you did for Jairus, his servant and the entire family, in the name of Jesus Christ, amen.

As Desperate As Bartimaeus

Apart from the above two examples provided, namely, the man at the Pool of Bethesda and Jairus daughter, the third person who was in a state of despair and didn't let go, was Bartimaeus. He had a choice to keep quiet as advised by the public, but in his state of desperation the blind man chose to shout louder than the crowd who were boisterous and thronging around Jesus—the Miracle-worker. We should not be surprised about how rowdy and busy the environment could have been.

In today's world, we know that famous people or celebrities are crowd-pullers, but Jesus was more than a celebrity, or crowd-puller. He never conducted Himself as if He was a crowd-puller, yet, we can imagine the size of assemblage wherever He went to. In spite of the crowd of people who had surrounded the Son of God, Bartimaeus was undeterred, (Luke 18:35-43).

> Then it happened, as He was coming near Jericho, that a certain blind man sat by the road begging. 36 And hearing a multitude passing by, he asked what it meant. 37 So they told him that Jesus of Nazareth was passing by. 38 And he cried out, saying, "Jesus, Son of David, have mercy on me!" 39 Then those who went before warned him that he should be quiet; but he cried out all the more, "Son of David, have mercy on me!" 40 So Jesus stood still and commanded him to be brought to Him. And when he had come near, He asked him, 41 saying, "What do you want Me to do for you?" He said, "Lord, that I may receive my sight." 42 Then Jesus said to him, "Receive your sight; your faith has made you well." 43 And immediately he received his sight, and followed Him, glorifying God. And all the people, when they saw it, gave praise to God. Luke 18:35-43

By divine co-incidence Jesus heard Bartimaeus' voice, amazingly the charge from the opposition for him to be quiet did not discourage him and he was healed. What a turnaround! May God give you a voice when needed. You will never be discouraged all the days of your life. And may you be heard at the right time in the name of Jesus Christ, amen.

Was Jonah Ever Desperate?

In a characteristic fashion, God heard Jonah's voice during his crisis or moment of desperation, this God is wonderful. Bartimaeus called among the crowd of people who were commuting on the road, and Jesus heard his voice. Jonah called from inside the belly of a big fish which was lying at the seabed of an ocean, God still answered Jonah from there, (Jonah 2:1-2). Indeed He has proven by this that, He can hear His people wherever they call Him from. There is grace for you, receive it in the name of Jesus Christ.

> Then Jonah prayed to the LORD his God from the fish's belly. 2 And he said: "I cried out to the LORD because of my affliction, And He answered me. "Out of the belly of Sheol I cried, And You heard my voice. Jonah 2:1-2.

Let us recall that, Bartimaeus' voice rose above the gathering of people who surrounded him and his miracle took place. In a similar manner, the voice of Jonah rose from the belly of the big fish and echoed beyond the waves of the sea, then God commanded the big fish to take Jonah to the specific destination. May your voice echo towards heaven and fetch you miracles in the name of Jesus Christ.

What did the above mentioned three people (the man at Bethesda Pool, Jairus and Bartimaeus), do to merit their miracles? It was *charis,* a type of grace from God that we all need at times of despair. Note again, that Jairus, Bartimaeus and Jonah received their respective miracles because of *charis.* The assurance here is that, every believer can be heard as they call on God. He can hear us and can answer us whenever we pray, even right now.

Prayer Points

Uncommon grace from God, descend upon my life right now in the name of Jesus Christ

Every opposition confronting my consecration—prayer life, obedience to the word of God, and Bible study, all such oppositions terminate and be roasted by fire in the name of Jesus Christ

Every opposition confronting my fasting life, soul winning/ evangelism activity, tithing and giving to God's work, all such oppositions terminate and be roasted by fire in the name of Jesus Christ

Powers that oppose and confront marriage and fruitfulness, I am not your candidate, extinct and be roasted by fire in the name of Jesus Christ

Powers that oppose and confront finances and health, I am not your candidate, extinct and be roasted by fire in the name of Jesus Christ

Every opposition confronting my ministry and my fellow parishioners, terminate and be roasted by fire in the name of Jesus Christ

Every opposition confronting my ministry helpers and supporters, your time is over, terminate by fire and burn to ashes in the name of Jesus Christ

Every agenda of the wicked confronting my endeavours, terminate and be roasted by fire in the name of Jesus Christ

All opposition confronting my business and my other projects, terminate and be roasted by fire in the name of Jesus Christ

Every satanic voice speaking against the will of God for my life and family, be silenced forever in the name of Jesus Christ

My Father! Hear my prayers for my 'turnaround' from today, because of Your unfailing compassion in the name of Jesus Christ

Bartimaeus stood no chance, but by divine co-incidence something happened, say to the Lord, "Thou Son of David" have mercy on me from today and don't allow my life to remain the same

O God my Father! have mercy on me and let my life display your power and glory from today in the name of Jesus Christ

I receive mercy in the order of Bartimaeus, henceforth mercy shall locate me every day of my life, in the name of Jesus Christ

From today, I shall become a candidate of mercy, and will remain a recipient of mercy all the days of my life in the name of Jesus Christ

My Father, my Father, You gave Bartimaeus undeniable miracle and evidence, grant me my portion in the name of Jesus Christ

— Grant my spouse his/her portion
— Grant my children their portion
— Grant all my helpers their portion in the name of Jesus Christ

Jonah stood no chance at all, but by divine intervention, his voice rose above the waves of the ocean. My Father! Let all my prayers rise up to you and grant me speedy answers in the name of Jesus Christ

From today (mention your name, I, ...), I receive God's mercy in the order of Jonah, therefore, mercy shall locate me and my entire household every day in the name of Jesus Christ

(Mention your name, I,....................), from today, I receive God's mercy in the order of Jonah, and I shall become a candidate of mercy, and will remain a recipient of mercy all my entire life in the name of Jesus Christ, amen.

Extraordinary Grace, Or Grace Re-defined?

In all of the above three cited examples, where does Jonah fit in? Who solicited for him during his plight? Would it be appropriate to say Jonah was indifferent to his circumstance, didn't care about his own life, and was insensitive to the consequences the Ninevites might suffer? Was there an instance where he (Jonah) needed to cry to God by himself like Bartimaeus? Was there any justifiable reason for the grace which translated to mercy, to have been shown to Jonah? As biblically recorded, Jonah didn't shout like Bartimaeus, nor had someone go and fetch Jesus for him like Jairus did for his daughter.

But rather, it was God Himself who went to Jonah's rescue when he was thrown into the raging sea. We recall firstly that, God provided a big fish to house him. Secondly, God offered him a free transportation to Nineveh. And extraordinarily, like the man at the Pool of Bethesda where Jesus walked to the man in (John 5:1-8), God came to Jonah's rescue and He (God) completed the rest, as if grace was re-defined.

It is obvious that the runaway evangelist behaved badly from the beginning. The question is, should a runaway prophet remain in God's good books? Not only a runaway evangelist, but he also failed to be empathetic. How possible is it for someone with national hatred for the Assyrians, ingrained anger, and bitterness come before the Lord? I mean, the Holy God. Definitely, God had reserved some special mercy for Jonah as we shall see in the next chapter.

CHAPTER FIVE
SPECIAL MERCY FOR JONAH

What Is Your Opinion?

Many people would remember Jonah as the runaway prophet whom God sent on a missionary journey to a foreign land, precisely Nineveh, somewhere in the biblical Assyrian empire. Note that Nineveh is modern day Mosul in Iraq. During that time, Nineveh was a flourishing city with its boisterous lifestyle and corruption. Jonah, if he was supposed to be as gentle as dove, (Yonah: Hebrew for Dove), would have none of that nonsense, hence he came up with his plan—to escape to Tarshish.

Did Jonah deserved to be shown mercy in regards to the way he went about things initially, during and after? What did Jonah do to merit the mercy shown to him? Would God reward disobedience with kindness or favour? What can we make out of this man's itinerary?

But there are many Jonahs (fugitives) in today's world that we might not hear about, or lack information about them. Possibly, some might remember Jonah because of the way he was found sleeping in the lower deck of the ship that was heading to Tarshish, (Jonah 1:6). It may sound laughable, but in some parlance that I know, especially, among the Yoruba tribe in Nigeria, they sometimes refer to people as 'Jonah the sleeper' when caught sleeping at a time when they are not supposed to be sleeping. What a shame! Shamefully, it was a non-believer that told a man of God to go and pray, yet Jonah did not pray. As the Bible recorded,

So the captain came to him, and said to him, "What do you mean, sleeper? Arise, call on your God; perhaps your God will consider us, so that we may not perish."
Jonah 1:6

Hmm, the captain might be talking to any of my readers right now about their neglected social, financial, spiritual, economic, and parental duties, or what you have failed to do in the house of God. What choice have you made recently about your spiritual life, the salvation of your soul, vocation, education, finances, marriage, and so on? Where is your life heading to, is it to Tarshish like Jonah?

One of life's lessons here is that, someone in the Christian faith might be sleeping spiritually now, or possibly not living up to the required standards of their position or calling. The irony is that, if God's children fail to live up to the expected standards, to their shame, unbelievers or the unsaved like the 'captain' will rebuke them exactly like the mariner did to Jonah. I pray that, we all shall live up to the expected standards as desired by God for us.

At the time, it was a deliberate choice that Jonah made to go the opposite direction. He was bent on refusing the divine assignment God gave to him. Nowadays, there are many people who have decided to go the opposite direction in life due to issues beyond their control. For such, they need prayers and I pray that the mighty hand of God would snatch them from the clutches of Satan and his forces, and set God's children free in the name of Jesus Christ.

And for those who have refused the call to go to their 'Nineveh' where God has assigned to them, my prayer is that they won't learn in a hard way. That sooner than later, they would repent because the Bible says, it is a fearful thing to fall into the hands of the living God, (Hebrews 10:31). If God is calling you to a particular area of ministry, business, or to learn a trade, do not hesitate because your disobedience can attract terrible consequences. Some few lessons can be learned from Jonah's temperament as we shall soon find out in this publication.

The Storm at Sea

The raging of the sea began unexpectedly and the suddenness caused the seasoned mariners and other travellers to panic, be in fear of their lives, and desperately needed urgent solution which was not available. How the sailors despite their experience, and the travellers wished the storm ceased suddenly the way it had began! Unfortunately, that was not the case. Regrettably, the sailors and the traders on-board had to throw away some of their merchandise to reduce the weight of the ship.

In their mind, the mariners who were likely Phoenicians who knew the way of the sea professionally, had thought that making the ship lighter would help to steady the vessel and keep it afloat. Alas, they were wrong, it got worse and there was a secret they were yet to uncover. Jonah was the secret and the problem. Pray like this:

Almighty Father, deliver me from individuals who can cause difficulties (financial, material and spiritual) in my life, in the name of Jesus Christ

— Deliver me O Lord, in the name of Jesus Christ

Almighty Father, deliver me from individuals who can cause economic wastage to my livelihood and family in the name of Jesus Christ

— Deliver me O Lord, in the name of Jesus Christ

If you are an employer of labour, pray like this: Father, do not allow me to hire the services of a staff that would wreck my business in the name of Jesus Christ

Father, prevent me from hiring the services of problematic staff in the name of Jesus

Jehovah my Deliverer, deliver me from people who can sink and waste my resources, skill, talent and time in business, in the name of Jesus Christ

Jehovah my Deliverer, deliver me from people who can sink and waste my resources, skill, talent and time in ministry in the name of Jesus Christ

Father God, no matter how gifted or talented they appear, deliver me from individuals who can sink and waste my resources (business, spiritual, material and financial), in the name of Jesus Christ

God my Deliverer! Deliver me from people who can sink and waste my resources and endeavour in the name of Jesus Christ

The Lord of hosts! deliver me from satanic agents assigned to sink and waste my investment in life in the name of Jesus Christ

Jehovah—Thou Storm Stopper! Deliver me from all agents of Satan who can attract storm and wastage into my life and ministry in the name of Jesus

Every storm and wastage stop, and let my testimony appear in the name of Jesus

Every storm and wastage stop, and let God do something new in my life, in the name of Jesus

Rock of Ages, deliver me from agents of Satan assigned to capsize the 'ship' of my ministry in the name of Jesus Christ

Rock of Ages, collide with all satanic agents confronting my life and hand me victory

Thou Great Deliverer! collide with all satanic agents confronting my calling and hand me victory in the name of Jesus

Rock of Ages, deliver me from agents of Satan assigned to capsize the 'ship' of my business in the name of Jesus Christ

The Everlasting Arm of God! deliver me from agents of Satan assigned to capsize the 'ship' of my marriage in the name of Jesus Christ

Eternal Father, deliver me from agents of Satan assigned to capsize the 'ship' of my endeavours in the name of Jesus Christ

— Deliver me my Father, in the name of Jesus Christ

My Father and Defender! Deliver me from agents of Satan who can cause misfortune to any aspect of my life in the name of Jesus Christ

Mighty Father, deliver me from individuals who can sabotage the journey of my life in the name of Jesus Christ, amen.

No Room, And No Time For Prayer

When people sleep instead of staying awake and pray, that could be the beginning of their trouble, awake O sleeper! Imagine a world where Jonah didn't know how to swim, and if he did, how far would he be able to swim for in a stormy sea? Could a village or city be nearby to swim to, for a refuge? Not likely, what a dilemma! Worst of all, as a man of God, Jonah did not offer any prayers to God prior, and when he asked to be thrown into the sea—there is no record to show that he prayed. I know some of us would have prayed almost every prayer they knew how to, quote many scriptures that they could, cast and bind all the 'bindables' so that they wouldn't be drowned in the sea.

Shockingly, all the travellers didn't pray to God to still the storm—no room and there was no time for prayers. Rather, they were looking for the culprit, or the individual who brought 'bad luck' to them and the lot fell on Jonah, (Jonah 1:7).

And they said to one another, "Come, let us cast lots, that we may know for whose cause this trouble has come upon us." So they cast lots, and the lot fell on Jonah. Jonah 1:7

Respectfully speaking, I am a man of prayer, but from human perspective their immediate priority was getting the ship sailing and to be able to continue with their journey. I pray that from today, you will do the right thing at the right time, with the right people and get the legitimate results in the name of Jesus Christ.

Realistically, it was God who decided to tamper justice with mercy if not, Jonah would be dead by now. Further, none of the sailors cared about Jonah's condition and well-being and that is human being for you. Think about it, not a single person among the mariners cared if Jonah would be dead, or remained alive once thrown into the violent sea. Jonah himself would have thought death was inevitable. One of the moral lessons here is that, God is the only One who can genuinely care for you as stated in His word, (1 Peter 5:7),

> Casting all your care upon Him, for He cares for you.
> 1 Peter 5:7

Another lesson is that, in life it is possible to forget to pray when faced by imminent dangers, therefore, let prayer be your lifestyle so that there can be a 'reservoir' to draw from when the occasion demands for it—Pray without ceasing, (1 Thessalonians 5:17). My wish for you is that, faced by any challenge or issues of life, you will remember to pray to God for help, the One who said, "Call upon Me in the day of trouble; I will deliver you," (Psalm 50:15), may He answer and strengthen you from heaven in the name of Jesus Christ, (Psalm 20:1-2),

> May the LORD answer you in the day of trouble; May the name of the God of Jacob defend you; 2 May He send you help from the sanctuary, And strengthen you out of Zion. Psalm 20:1-2

> Call upon Me in the day of trouble; I will deliver you, and you shall glorify Me." Psalm 50:15

When The Storm Is From God, What Do You Say?

Let us consider two instances where God was behind the storm which was sent to two different characters. The first person was the runner-away Evangelist who knew God sent the storm because of his (Jonah) disobedience. Read Jonah 1:4,12-13,

"But the LORD sent out a great wind on the sea, and there was a mighty tempest on the sea, so that the ship was about to be broken up."... 12 And he (Jonah) said to them, "Pick me up and throw me into the sea; then the sea will become calm for you. For I know that this great tempest is because of me." Jonah 1:4, 12-13

As for the second person, God had held a discussion in the Council of Heaven and boasted to Satan that Job would not deny Him (God). But Satan objected, Read Job 1:8-12,

"Then the LORD said to Satan, "Have you considered My servant Job, that there is none like him on the earth, a blameless and upright man, one who fears God and shuns evil?" 9 So Satan answered the LORD and said, "Does Job fear God for nothing? 10 Have You not made a hedge around him, around his household, and around all that he has on every side? You have blessed the work of his hands, and his possessions have increased in the land. 11 But now, stretch out Your hand and touch all that he has, and he will surely curse You to Your face!" 12 And the LORD said to Satan, "Behold, all that he has is in your power; only do not lay a hand on his person." So Satan went out from the presence of the LORD." Job 1:8-12

As in the above two cases, God can be at work even when what is happening appears to be strange, challenging, caught you unprepared, is dangerous and extremely negative. Many times you may not have any clue. Why did I say that? To those who are not strong believers in the Christian faith, it might not make sense to them when God sent the great wind during Jonah's abortive journey, (Jonah 1:4), or when God allowed all the sons and daughters of Job to die, and the entire business to collapse all in one day, (Job 1:13-22).

63

Now there was a day when his sons and daughters were eating and drinking wine in their oldest brother's house; 14 and a messenger came to Job and said, "The oxen were plowing and the donkeys feeding beside them, 15 when the Sabeans raided them and took them away—indeed they have killed the servants with the edge of the sword; and I alone have escaped to tell you!" 16 While he was still speaking, another also came and said, "The fire of God fell from heaven and burned up the sheep and the servants, and consumed them; and I alone have escaped to tell you!" 17 While he was still speaking, another also came and said, "The Chaldeans formed three bands, raided the camels and took them away, yes, and killed the servants with the edge of the sword; and I alone have escaped to tell you!" 18 While he was still speaking, another also came and said, "Your sons and daughters were eating and drinking wine in their oldest brother's house, 19 and suddenly a great wind came from across the wilderness and struck the four corners of the house, and it fell on the young people, and they are dead; and I alone have escaped to tell you!" 20 Then Job arose, tore his robe, and shaved his head; and he fell to the ground and worshiped. 21 And he said: "Naked I came from my mother's womb, And naked shall I return there. The LORD gave, and the LORD has taken away; Blessed be the name of the LORD." 22 In all this Job did not sin nor charge God with wrong. Job 1:13-22

If Job's case was many years ago, what do you say when a Nigerian veteran in the faith, Reverend Dr. Uma Ukpai in one day lost all his office equipment and the printing machine, despite the corporate fasting and prayers they had offered to God who forewarned him. As if that was not enough, on the same day that he had a robbery incident, he travelled with his family and the driver who was driving the children's car lost control at the wheels and they fell into a river. Unfortunately, the children and other fatalities followed as published in the Punch Newspapers on 14/03/2015, and in Reverend Dr Uma's article on their website. He stated,

"On our way to a crusade in my village, my driver carrying my children and a cousin drove into a river. I attempted to bring the children out, not knowing that my wife also jumped into the river behind me and the water carried her, threw her up six times. It was at the seventh time that somebody called my attention to her. I used one hand to swim and the other to hold her and brought her to shore. I rescued the children later. They had died; because a child stays under water only for two minutes. I put them in a car to pray for them, but an oncoming car from the opposite direction drove into the car and smashed it. The bumper flew out, the bonnet flew out. I stopped and I was pacing up and down, not knowing what to do next.

Just then, somebody ran to me, grabbed me and said my 50-seater bus carrying my band had caught fire. He was not sure how many people died in the accident. I was composed because God had warned me. I didn't make those children. God gave them to me. All that I had, now have and will ever have is given by God. And His will is supreme. When I proceeded to the crusade venue to preach, people were asking me what will you preach? We have been driving on that same road for years and that driver had been my driver. If God, over the years, protected us and decided to lower the hedge one day, why should I protest? So, I marched on!

But I was shocked in 1982 while preparing for Greater Ibadan for Christ Crusade, God said to me, for handling that case well, you will be seen everywhere. He said; I will detail 100 angels to be with you wherever you go in the world."[7]

This God is indescribable in that He allowed the storm, it came from Him. For short, when the storm is from God, continue to serve Him like Reverend Dr Uma Ukpai has been doing. His story has encouraged me to serve God without looking back when I lost my twenty three year old son on 22/07/2021, he was not sick but went to be with the Lord from his sleep. The incident beats my imagination till the time of writing this manuscript. He was home for his University holiday and we joked about the Covid-19 Test I was going to do on that day, and when I returned with the sister about four or five hours later, he had passed—just like that? It is not about me but God. Without doubt, God was the One behind it and He knew the purpose He wanted to accomplish for everything. The good news is that as soon as His intention is achieved, like in all other stories cited in this book, He caused the storm to cease for Reverend Dr Uma Ukpai and Jonah, (Jonah 1:15), and me too. Let every storm in your life cease in the name of Jesus of Nazareth.

Then they picked up Jonah and threw him overboard into the raging sea—and the storm stopped! Jonah 1:15 TLB

---

7   https://www.thecomfortzone.se/god-doesnt-answer-dr-uma-ukpai/ Cited 01/05/2025

There is a reader of this book who needs to be encouraged, realise that God was behind what Pharaoh did to the Israelites. What about Job? He was a man of integrity and he terribly feared God, yet God was behind his plight. However, as soon as God's purpose was established, he (Job) was restored, (Job 42:12-17).

> Now the LORD blessed the latter days of Job more than his beginning; for he had fourteen thousand sheep, six thousand camels, one thousand yoke of oxen, and one thousand female donkeys. 13 He also had seven sons and three daughters. 14 And he called the name of the first Jemimah, the name of the second Keziah, and the name of the third Keren-Happuch. 15 In all the land were found no women so beautiful as the daughters of Job; and their father gave them an inheritance among their brothers. 16 After this Job lived one hundred and forty years, and saw his children and grandchildren for four generations. 17 So Job died, old and full of days. Job 42:12-17

My prayer for you is that, the Lord will grant you the strength you require to stand any ordeal that comes, restore and spare your life, and let His purpose for your life be established sooner than later.

Remember, God did it for Jonah and Reverend Dr Uma Ukpai, and He is helping me too. He will see you through every storm in your life because of His mercy, and your story shall end well. God's reason for allowing you to go through the challenges you are facing will be established quickly, and the storm shall cease abruptly, and permanently in the name of Jesus Christ. The Lord shall make you arrive safely at your "Nineveh"—your place of assignment and manifestation. I want you to realise that God was behind what Pharaoh did to the Israelites. What about Job? He was a man of integrity and terribly feared God, yet God was behind his plight. Be assured, there's mercy incomparable—mercy like no other, available to you as discussed in the next chapter. You will fulfil your destiny and God's name shall be glorified. God will do miracles to make you know that there's nothing compared to mercy, mercy like no other for you, and He will grant you grace to possess all your possessions, amen.

CHAPTER SIX
MERCY LIKE NO OTHER

Search Your Heart

Have you heard about people doing the wrong things when not expected of them? Jonah was caught in the act—he disobeyed God by heading to Tarshish (Jonah 1:3).

> But Jonah arose to flee to Tarshish from the presence of the LORD. He went down to Joppa, and found a ship going to Tarshish; so he paid the fare, and went down into it, to go with them to Tarshish from the presence of the LORD. Jonah 1:3

As if that was not enough, Jonah was caught sleeping by the non-Jewish captain (Jonah 1:6). The question is, why should God be merciful to him?

> So the captain came to him, and said to him, "What do you mean, sleeper? Arise, call on your God; perhaps your God will consider us, so that we may not perish." Jonah 1:6

Why was Jonah fast asleep? Was it due to ordinary tiredness, fatigue, or sleepiness due to exhaustion after running helter-skelter? Was it a divinely induced sleep to bring honour and glory to God? Or something to teach us some life's lessons? Clearly, there are things which can surpass our understanding and reasoning, but not God. In another way, was that a case of someone being spiritually asleep, and needs re-awakening? Supposing that 'Jonah' to be yourself, a member, or a head of your church, would you avoid or gossip him or her? Would you have walked away? What do you think God's response should be, or should have been? As yet, we may lack all the necessary tools, but there is nothing that can evade God's understanding, power and decision in this matter. He alone can do great and marvellous things as recorded in (Job 5:8-9; 37:5). Therefore, we should not be surprised when God decided to be merciful to Jonah—as if God lacked other people He could show mercy to. It was mercy like no other that was in operation at the time.

> But as for me, I would seek God, And to God I would commit my cause—9 Who does great things, and unsearchable, Marvellous things without number. Job 5:8-9

> God thunders marvellously with His voice; He does great things which we cannot comprehend. Job 37:5

As part of God's mercy which was shown to Jonah, He (God) created a safety device that was perfect for the extraordinary situation that Jonah found himself in—a great fish, (Jonah 1:17).

> Now the Lord had arranged for a great fish to swallow Jonah. And Jonah was inside the fish three days and three nights. Jonah 1:17 TLB

Succinctly, the merciful God was at work in spite of Jonah's behaviour and He spared Jonah. Was God under any contract to make such arrangements? Emphatic NO. Simply, mercy located Jonah wherever he was at the time. May the mercy of God locate you and all your loved ones today. As we ponder on Jonah's story, it is appropriate to say that, it was mercy like no other, that has began to unfold before our eyes, and it is beyond human understanding.

Why? Because all the necessary arrangements were already in place such that, the big fish that would convey Jonah to Nineveh was parked like a car in a garage, sitting at the bottom of the sea and waiting for him to come and board it. By that provision, God had prevented Jonah from drowning or facing accidental death. May you walk into your miracles from today in the name of Jesus Christ. May your spouse and your entire family walk into their miracles in the name of Jesus Christ.

Again, it was an act of mercy on God's part that prevented the digestive system of the whale from digesting Jonah like food material while in its belly. Normally, by the third day and third night, there supposed to be a dead man in the belly of the big fish, for example, due to the loss of oxygen. But Jonah was spared, exactly as Daniel was not meant to be meat for the lions in the den, Daniel 6:21-22,

> Then Daniel said to the king, "O king, live forever! 22 My God sent His angel and shut the lions' mouths, so that they have not hurt me, because I was found innocent before Him; and also, O king, I have done no wrong before you." Daniel 6:19-22

Who was responsible for that? It was God. May you and your entire family be preserved through the mercies of God in the name of Jesus of Nazareth. May God, who preserved Jonah despite his disobedience and sleepiness, be merciful to you, and preserve you. God will not allow you to be consumed by the wicked 'whales' or 'lions' of this world. Certainly, as the Bible states, it is through God's mercies we are not consumed, (Lamentation 3:22), you and your entire family will not be consumed in the name of Jesus Christ.

Prayer Points

Father of the fatherless, deliver me and my family from any type of accidental death in the name of Jesus Christ

Father, deliver me and my family from any type of premature death in the name of Jesus Christ

Merciful Father, deliver me and my family from any type of untimely death in the name of Jesus Christ

Father, deliver me and my family from sudden death in the name of Jesus Christ

Great Deliverer, don't allow disobedience send me to death before my time in the name of Jesus Christ

O Lord, deliver me and all my loved ones from untimely death in the name of Jesus Christ

Faithful Father, don't let me sleep the sleep of death. Don't allow any member of my family to sleep the sleep of death. Don't allow any of my loved ones to sleep the sleep of death, in the name of Jesus Christ, amen.

Breaking Natural Laws As If They Are Nothing

Humans are limited in scope and their abilities. They are bound by natural order and laws, but God can suspend, break, reset, or re-arrange them to make His will to happen as He intended. We remember how Jesus walked on water by suspending the law of gravity. But, the way in which God dealt with Jonah was completely different. Let us cast our minds back to the time when the storm ceased. Why should the storm cease when Jonah was thrown into the sea? Why should a big fish (as if an underwater ship), be on the exact spot where Jonah was thrown into?

Let's recap, we read from the biblical account that Jonah was meant to go to Nineveh, but how did the big fish know where to ferry Jonah, and vomit him out as if they both made a prior arrangement for Jonah to embark at mid-sea and disembark at Nineveh's beach?

Here is the clue, because of mercy like no other, God spoke to the fish as recorded in (Jonah 2:10), but Jonah was not aware of that. What type of dialogue could have ensued between the fish and God? How was Jonah able to get some oxygen to fill his lungs to survive the three days and three nights ordeal? Did Jonah communicate with the big fish by himself? NO. It was entirely God's idea. Simply, God worked out everything because of mercy which is incomparable to any other. May you became a candidate of mercy from today in the name of Jesus Christ of Nazareth.

Was Jonah in a coma or died, and then God raised him like Jesus did to Lazarus? My inclination is, God suspended every natural order or law we would ever know or think of, to preserve Jonah and to ensure that His (God's) will was done. May God's will be done in the lives of all my readers. What made God go to this extent? It was because of mercy.

Prayer Points

Father of mercy and grace, have mercy on me

Have mercy on my spouse

Have mercy on my entire family

Have mercy on my siblings

Have mercy on my ministry in the name of Jesus Christ

Have mercy on my business in the name of Jesus Christ

Have mercy on my career in the name of Jesus Christ

My Father, re-order every natural law hindering me, and let your perfect will, to be done in my life in the name of Jesus Christ

Almighty God, You suspended all natural laws for Jonah to be preserved, suspend all natural laws for me, and let my life be precious in your sight in the name of Jesus Christ

— Let my destiny be precious in your sight in the name of Jesus Christ
— Let my calling be precious in your sight in the name of Jesus Christ
— Let my all my aspirations be precious in your sight in the name of Jesus Christ

Merciful God, suspend all natural laws, preserve, and bless my family in the name of Jesus Christ

O Shepherd of Israel, suspend all natural laws and preserve my ministry in the name of Jesus

Stone of Israel, suspend all natural laws and preserve my business in the name of Jesus

Stone of Israel, suspend all natural laws and preserve my career in the name of Jesus

Almighty Father, suspend all natural laws and preserve all my endeavours in the name of Jesus Christ, amen.

Mount Carmel, The Mountain Of Fire

Talking about suspending natural laws, another typical example that comes to mind is the competition on Muhraka. That highest tip of the stretch of the mountain (Carmel) remains an extraordinary reminder about the ministry of Elijah, and how the power of God was demonstrated there on Mount Carmel. It was on this mountain that Elijah prayed for fire to fall from heaven and the fire fell and consumed his sacrifice which he offered to God, (1 Kings 18:38). His ministry which characteristically was vibrant and ruthless towards Baal prophets, and the idolatrous Israel at the time, needed such peculiar spiritual action, and God obliged him. The intervention was supernaturally phenomenal. May God intervene practically and tangibly in your life beginning from now.

Unbelievably, it was the fire that licked up the water and other items Elijah arranged for the sacrifice on the prepared altar. Did the fire lick up the water instead of quenching it? YES. The water burned like a fuel (petrol) to the amazement of all the people there. It is not an exaggeration to say that the natural or science order was reversed or broken by God on that day, (1 Kings 18:38). And because the natural law was either reversed, broken, or suspended, the heart of the people was turned to God from their idolatrous worship as they shouted excitedly, "the LORD, He is God," (1 Kings 18:39). Let us read,

> Then the fire of the LORD fell, and consumed the burnt sacrifice, and the wood, and the stones, and the dust, and licked up the water that was in the trench. 39 Now

when all the people saw it, they fell on their faces; and they said, "The LORD, He is God! The LORD, He is God!" 1 Kings 18:38-39

The Symbol/Pattern Of Fire

• Joy and deep worship

As a result of the role of fire in the contest on Mount Carmel, it is important to discuss briefly, the pattern of fire wherever you find them in the Bible. Fire in the biblical account could mean a lot, but a few of them would be discussed in this subsection. It was usual to see fire come from God's presence to accomplish several purposes which included joy and deep worship as in (Leviticus 9:24).

> And Moses and Aaron went into the tabernacle of meeting, and came out and blessed the people. Then the glory of the LORD appeared to all the people, 24 and fire came out from before the LORD and consumed the burnt offering and the fat on the altar. When all the people saw it, they shouted and fell on their faces. Leviticus 9:23-24

The above text confirms that the tangible presence of God in form of fire, fell on the children of Israel when Moses and Aaron appeared from the place of meeting. While this happened, the instant response on the part of the Israelites was, they shouted for joy and prostrated in worship. The challenge for us today is how can we attract God's 'fire' regularly, and what should be our response?

Have our priorities changed? Do we have passion for the 'fire' at the moment? But we need the 'fire' badly now.

Where are the "Moseses" and "Aarons" among us who can attract the 'fire' for us again? Let them come out, if not, what can be done? Who is ready to pay the price? Have we all become lukewarm or languid? Pray like this:

Father, ignite your 'fire' afresh in me in the name of Jesus Christ

— Ignite your fire afresh in my family
— Ignite your 'fire' afresh in my community, ministry and in all my endeavours in the name of Jesus Christ

Fire of God that produces joy, I am available, descend afresh on me today in the name of Jesus Christ

— Descend afresh upon my spouse and my entire family
— Descend afresh on my ministry and business and all my endeavours in the name of Jesus Christ, amen.

• Confirmation that your sacrifices have been accepted

Another purpose that the fire of God serves is to convince His children that their sacrifices have been accepted at certain crucial moments in their lives (Judges 6:19-24).

> So Gideon went in and prepared a young goat, and unleavened bread from an ephah of flour. The meat he put in a basket, and he put the broth in a pot; and he brought them out to Him under the terebinth tree and presented them. 20 The Angel of God said to him, "Take the meat and the unleavened bread and lay them on this rock, and pour out the broth." And he did so. 21 Then the Angel of the LORD put out the end of the staff that was in His hand, and touched the meat and the unleavened bread; and fire rose out of the rock and

consumed the meat and the unleavened bread. And the Angel of the LORD departed out of his sight. 22 Now Gideon perceived that He was the Angel of the LORD. So Gideon said, "Alas, O Lord GOD! For I have seen the Angel of the LORD face to face." 23 Then the LORD said to him, "Peace be with you; do not fear, you shall not die." 24 So Gideon built an altar there to the LORD, and called it The-LORD-Is-Peace. To this day it is still in Ophrah of the Abiezrites. Judges 6:19-24

As in the above text, Gideon was fearful, timid and inexperienced, and he was hesitant to assume the role of a military leader, and deliverer of God's people. Typically, he reminds us about Moses who tendered excuses but in the end, accepted the call and the commission, (Exodus 3:11; 4:10-14, 18).

But Moses said to God, "Who am I that I should go to Pharaoh, and that I should bring the children of Israel out of Egypt?" Exodus 3:11

Then Moses said to the LORD, "O my Lord, I am not eloquent, neither before nor since You have spoken to Your servant; but I am slow of speech and slow of tongue." 11 So the LORD said to him, "Who has made man's mouth? Or who makes the mute, the deaf, the seeing, or the blind? Have not I, the LORD? 12 Now therefore, go, and I will be with your mouth and teach you what you shall say." 13 But he said, "O my Lord, please send by the hand of whomever else You may send." 14 So the anger of the LORD was kindled against Moses, and He said: "Is not Aaron the Levite your brother? I know that he can speak well. And look, he is also coming out to meet you. When he sees you, he will be glad in his heart ... 18 So Moses went and returned to Jethro his father-in-law, and said to him, "Please let me go and return to my brethren who are in Egypt, and see whether they are still alive." And Jethro said to Moses, "Go in peace." Exodus 4:10-14, 18

However, Gideon later became a man of faith, then he was called and commissioned. Soon he built an altar to the LORD, (Judges 6:24).

So Gideon built an altar there to the LORD, and called it The-Lord-Is-Peace. To this day it is still in Ophrah of the Abiezrites. Judges 6:24

Furthermore, Gideon was emboldened to pull down and destroy the altar of Baal, and he did as instructed, (Judges 6:27). let us read,

So Gideon took ten men from among his servants and did as the LORD had said to him. But because he feared his father's household and the men of the city too much to do it by day, he did it by night. Judges 6:27

Note, God had to convince Gideon by using the sign of fire as stated in (Judges 6:21-22). May God give you what I call 'a covenant sign' that would help you to connect with destiny, and make you become the person He has created you to be, in the name of Jesus Christ.

Then the Angel of the LORD put out the end of the staff that was in His hand, and touched the meat and the unleavened bread; and fire rose out of the rock and consumed the meat and the unleavened bread. And the Angel of the LORD departed out of his sight. 22 Now Gideon perceived that He was the Angel of the LORD. So Gideon said, "Alas, O Lord GOD! For I have seen the Angel of the LORD face to face." Judges 6:21-22

• To motivate and inspire you for destiny assignment

Additionally, one of the purposes that fire of God serves, as we learn from Gideon's encounter is to motivate and inspire individuals to step into their destiny assignment. Pray like this,

My Father, my Father, settle my case by fire!

My Father, my Father, help me to step into my destiny assignment from today in the name of Jesus Christ, amen.

To conclude the subsection titled, the pattern/symbol of fire, another important and unforgettable experience occurred in the New Testament. This happened fifty days after the crucifixion of Jesus Christ. By that I refer to what happened in (Acts 2:1-3), where divided tongues like fire sat upon God's people to accomplish a special purpose in believers lives. It should be understood that the fire represents the purifying presence of God that burns all undesirable elements in the lives of believers. As it did in the past, so it can do now, and always. May God accomplish extraordinary things in your life from today. Let us read,

> When the Day of Pentecost had fully come, they were all with one accord in one place. 2 And suddenly there came a sound from heaven, as of a rushing mighty wind, and it filled the whole house where they were sitting. 3 Then there appeared to them divided tongues, as of fire, and one sat upon each of them. Acts 2:1-3

Always Remember The Golden Rule

Having discussed a little about the pattern or symbolism of fire, let us turn our attention to Jonah again. One thing is clear, we are swift to condemn people, but a lot of times we should learn to put ourselves in the other person's shoes. That is, be empathetic. Further, we might be quick to conclude, but God didn't do that to Jonah, instead He showed him abundant mercies. It is important to not take God for granted as He does what pleases Him, including the decision and His choice of the one to show mercy to, or compassion—the mercies of God come to those He chooses as declared in (Exodus 33:19b), let us confirm,

> I will be gracious to whom I will be gracious, and I will have compassion on whom I will have compassion. Exodus 33:19b

Instead of condemning or judging, it is wise to ask for God's mercies in all forms and shapes, and in the most appropriate way to meet one's needs, because like Jonah, there will come a time in one's life that you won't be in control. But it is encouraging to know that God's mercy is abundant and infinite in measure, limitless in comparison, and it is great and beyond description as expressed in (Psalm 103:11). Let us read,

> For as the heaven is high above the earth, so great is his mercy toward them that fear him. Psalm 103:11

Amazingly, and the most important of all, the mercy of God is new each day, (Lamentation 3:22-23),

> It is of the LORD's mercies that we are not consumed, because his compassions fail not. 23 They are new

every morning: great is thy faithfulness. Lamentation 3:22-23

The Three Dimensions Of The Universality of God's Mercies

God's mercy is universal in nature and can be seen in the following three ways specifically in the Book of Jonah.

1. Because of the universal nature of mercy, God related with Jonah on a one-on-one basis. There was no other person (an intermediary) between the two of them, even when it appeared like the worst moment between the two of them had come, yet God would speak with Jonah directly once He was ready.

This same God is ready to associate with any of His children on a one-on-one basis. He is ready to do so with their family, ministry, business, education, and in all their entire lives. Also, that God's mercies can be individualised as seen from how He patiently related with Jonah on a personal level from the time he was called, sent him to Nineveh, God endured and tolerated Jonah while behaving disobediently against His instruction, even when Jonah relapsed in faith and wished for death to take him, God didn't relent until Jonah was restored.

2. Because of the universal nature of God's mercy, victims of circumstance can be redeemed from their troubles, without realising it. How do I mean? As we read in the book of Jonah, because of mercy, God responded to the appeal of the mariners who were victims of a circumstance. It seems they didn't pray to the God of Israel, yet He rescued them. Furthermore,

they were non-Israelites, not part of the covenanted nation of Israel, but Yahweh calmed the sea for the sailors, and did not allow their ship to wreck or break during the violent storm.

3. God can grant a special pardon and many more, to the undeserved because of the universal nature of His mercy. How possible some might ask? Here is what God did: through His mercies Jonah was not abandoned, the Ninevites were spared the pending wrath and God's judgment after they had fasted and repented. By this act we can conclude that the undeserved received a special pardon from God.

But remember, you have read about the uniqueness of Jonah's call and commission, the special mercy which is incomparable to any type. This same God is ready to work with you. Suffice to say that, God who was there for the people of Israel throughout the Old Testament period, was there for the Ninevites, is still available to all Christian believers of today, hallelujah! And if you are still wondering about the universality of God's mercies, there is one more thing to join in the mix, or network, it is the big fish—God used it to ferry Jonah to a safe place, more on this in the next chapter.

CHAPTER SEVEN
JONAH, THE NINEVITES AND THE BIG FISH

Jonah And The Ninevites Mix

Jonah was one of the prophets of Israel who was sent to preach at Nineveh, the Assyrian capital of the time. Why was that? God wanted them to repent of their evil ways, which included, lies, rape, sorcery, harlotry, witchcraft and seduction of other nations, violence and wasting of lives, Jonah 3:5-10,

So the people of Nineveh believed God, proclaimed a fast, and put on sackcloth, from the greatest to the least of them. 6 Then word came to the king of Nineveh; and he arose from his throne and laid aside his robe, covered himself with sackcloth and sat in ashes. 7 And he caused it to be proclaimed and published throughout Nineveh by the decree of the king and his nobles, saying, Let neither man nor beast, herd nor flock, taste anything; do not let them eat, or drink water. 8 But let man and beast be covered with sackcloth, and cry mightily to God; yes, let every one turn from his evil way and from the violence that is in his hands. 9 Who can tell if God will turn and relent, and turn away from His fierce anger, so that we may not perish? 10 Then God saw their works, that they turned from their evil way; and God relented from the disaster that He had said He would bring upon them, and He did not do it. Jonah 3:5-10

As it happened, God forgave them and relented and did not execute the intended judgment of destruction because they repented. Interestingly, Jonah initially did not want to go and preach to them, instead he decided to run away. His and the Ninevites case was like an entanglement or a mix, which was difficult to disengage or separate from one another. Of these two categories of people, it is pertinent to ask, who deserved to be spared, the reluctant prophet with racist attitude, or the Ninevites who were deep in evil ways? Thankfully, Jonah realised his mistake sooner.

Remember that God spared Jonah who ran away from the missional duty that was assigned to him. Further, this same God forgave the people of Nineveh, despite the wickedness and atrocities they caused their neighbours. In addition, God had compassion on them, that is, all the inhabitants of Nineveh and Jonah too. Only God's mercies could have been the motivation for this kind gesture. Would Jonah learn to show mercy on others as he was shown? Not really.

Typically, we can be reminded about the forgiven-debtor who refused to forgive a fellow debtor. If God would hold any person to account, how many people do you think would be judged because of failure to show mercy on others? I want to refer to (Matthew 18:27-34). Let us read,

> Then the lord of that servant was moved with compassion, and loosed him, and forgave him the debt. 28 But the same servant went out, and found one of his fellowservants, which owed him an hundred pence: and he laid hands on him, and took him by the throat, saying, Pay me that thou owest. 29 And his fellowservant fell down at his feet, and besought him, saying, Have patience with me, and I will pay thee all. 30 And he would not: but went and cast him into prison, till he

should pay the debt. 31 So when his fellowservants saw what was done, they were very sorry, and came and told unto their lord all that was done. 32 Then his lord, after that he had called him, said unto him, O thou wicked servant, I forgave thee all that debt, because thou desiredst me: 33 shouldest not thou also have had compassion on thy fellowservant, even as I had pity on thee? 34 And his lord was wroth, and delivered him to the tormentors, till he should pay all that was due unto him. Matthew 18:27-34 AV

How are Christian believers supposed to respond to one another in regards to showing kindness, mercy, forgiveness and so on? In context, the above scripture was about forgiveness or pardon extended to a debtor/sinner, and the expectation was that the forgiven individual, would extend compassion and grace to others which unfortunately, is not always the case.

In real life, and I agree with an eminent scholar that, remaining merciless and unforgiving within the text was ludicrous in light of God's incalculable grace on us.[8] Perhaps, we would never know how many people have been, or would be caught in this type of situation in today's world. It is unbelievable, but true that Jonah who was forgiven as a runaway evangelist and prophet, if possible would not have forgiven the Ninevites, even when it was within his power to do so.

You Can Run, But You Cannot Hide

The question is, can anyone disappear from God's sight, become undetectable, or run out of God's reach? Jonah's

---

8 R. T France, Contribution on Matthew in New Bible Commentary, 21st Century Edition, Leicester, England: Inter-Varsity Press, 1994, p. 929

attempt to run away from what God told him to do seems to be a very good test-case. But what is amazing is, in the end God's mercy was expended on this individual who was once drowned but alive prophet. What about the inhabitants of Nineveh? Jonah and his countrymen anticipated God's judgment on the Assyrians during that time, but that was not God's plan for the Assyrians. This shows us how quickly but thoughtless, and inconsiderate some humans wish God's judgment fall on their fellows. Unfortunately for them, God remains compassionate to all. We may not understand, but most of the time, God's judgment doesn't happen or meet with our expectations. Can anyone understand why? Certainly, His thoughts are deep, and His ways are not our ways, as stated in (Psalm 92:5-6),

O LORD, how great are thy works! *and* thy thoughts are very deep. 6 A brutish man knoweth not; neither doth a fool understand this. Psalm 92:5-6 AV

Unknown to Jonah who once was a fugitive, but used prophet, as his anger was rising, (read Jonah 4:1-2), God's mercies was covering the wickedness and all the atrocities which was committed by the heathen inhabitants of the city of Nineveh, as narrated in (Jonah 4:10-11).

But it displeased Jonah exceedingly, and he was very angry. 2 And he prayed unto the LORD, and said, I pray thee, O LORD, was not this my saying, when I was yet in my country? Therefore I fled before unto Tarshish: for I knew that thou art a gracious God, and merciful, slow to anger, and of great kindness, and repentest thee of the evil. Jonah 4:1-2 AV

Then said the LORD, Thou hast had pity on the gourd, for the which thou hast not laboured, neither madest it grow; which came up in a night, and perished in a night: 11 and should not I spare Nineveh, that great city, wherein are more than sixscore thousand persons that cannot discern between their right hand and their left hand; and also much cattle? Jonah 4:10-11 AV

Jonah—What Story?

Some critics believe that this story is a parable, allegory, or mythology, even though Jonah's descendants can be traced to the tribe of Zebulun, (Joshua 19:10-13), and in (2 Kings 14:25-26).[9]

And the third lot came up for the children of Zebulun according to their families: and the border of their inheritance was unto Sarid: 11 and their border went up toward the sea, and Maralah, and reached to Dabbasheth, and reached to the river that *is* before Jokneam; 12 and turned from Sarid eastward toward the sunrising unto the border of Chisloth-tabor, and then goeth out to Daberath, and goeth up to Japhia, 13 and from thence passeth on along on the east to Gittah-hepher, to Ittah-kazin, and goeth out to Remmon-methoar to Neah. Joshua 19:10-13 AV

He restored the coast of Israel from the entering of Hamath unto the sea of the plain, according to the word of the LORD God of Israel, which he spake by the hand of his servant Jonah, the son of Amittai, the prophet, which was of Gath-hepher. 26 For the LORD saw the affliction of Israel, that it was very bitter: for there was not any shut up, nor any left, nor any helper for Israel. 2 Kings 14:25-26 AV

---

9 Derek Williams, (Ed.), New Concise Bible Dictionary, Leicester, England: Inter-Varsity Press, 1989, p.283

The sheer power of nature (the sea) and its consequential physical phenomenon when it rages, can be indescribable, yet it seems God decided to use the storm to get across to Jonah. How? As you have read already, God made the violent storm to rise fiercely and through casting of lots, it was discovered that Jonah was the reason for the chaos. As a result, he was thrown into the sea by the sailors and the storm ceased, (Jonah 1:13-16). As we read, is God trying to get across to you too? Why not seek His face prayerfully for you to know His will for your life?

> Nevertheless the men rowed hard to bring *it* to the land; but they could not: for the sea wrought, and was tempestuous against them. 14 Wherefore they cried unto the LORD, and said, We beseech thee, O LORD, we beseech thee, let us not perish for this man's life, and lay not upon us innocent blood: for thou, O LORD, hast done as it pleased thee. 15 So they took up Jonah, and cast him forth into the sea: and the sea ceased from her raging. 16 Then the men feared the LORD exceedingly, and offered a sacrifice unto the LORD, and made vows. Jonah 1:13-16 AV

The Big Fish

Whilst no thoughts was given about Jonah after the fierce storm had ceased, the mercy of God (Hebrew: *chesed*, that is, kindness/favour of God), still operated in Jonah's life again. How? God had prepared an escape route by which Jonah would be rescued by a big fish, see (Jonah 1:17; 2:10). There is a reader of this book who needs to be released from a "tight corner," the Lord shall make escape routes available to you in the name of Jesus Christ.

Now the LORD had prepared a great fish to swallow up
Jonah. And Jonah was in the belly of the fish three days
and three nights. Jonah 1:17 AV

And the LORD spake unto the fish, and it vomited out
Jonah upon the dry land. Jonah 2:10 AV

A Big Fish And The Ark Of Noah

In contrast, while the big fish was meant to transport Jonah to
Nineveh so that the souls of the heathens could be preserved,
it comes to mind how God had equally picked one man called
Noah in (Genesis 6:7-8), to save some of the people during his
time, but they refused to listen to him. While Jonah was
transported by a big fish, Noah, his family and other creatures
were transported in an Ark, (Genesis 7:23). One clear
intention by God in both cases is to save souls, even till now.

And every living substance was destroyed which was
upon the face of the ground, both man, and cattle, and
the creeping things, and the fowl of the heaven; and
they were destroyed from the earth: and Noah only
remained alive, and they that were with him in the ark.
Genesis 7:23 AV

Whether transported by a big fish or in an ark, God was
involved. May God be involved in all your issues in the name
of Jesus Christ. Note that the Ark was a typology or picture
of Christ and the water of the flood was the instrument
of judgment.[10] Although a destruction awaited the Ninevites
if they failed to repent, but the particular instrument of
judgment was not mentioned.

---

10 William MacDonald, Art Farstad (Ed.), Believer's Bible Commentary - A
Complete Bible Commentary in One Volume, London: Thomas Nelson
Publishers, 1995, p. 43

There is no intention to stir up a debate, or a comparison between the big fish and the Ark of Noah, because each of them carries their uniqueness and significance. Moving forward, the point that should concern us is that, the instrument of judgment should not be more important, but rather, we should be interested in how God finds different means and methods to save people from destruction, or His judgment.

In addition, there is no doubt that God keeps finding a way to deliver humanity from sin and eternal death. He can, and will continue to find a way for salvation of souls of human beings.

Who Will Believe Our Report?

What would Jonah be hoping for? Let us remember that God gave an opportunity to Jonah when he was in the belly of the big fish to remain alive. In a similar manner, the wicked inhabitants of the Assyrian capital were spared when they fasted and prayed, but Jonah was unhappy about God's decision.

So far, some critics never believed that a human can survive three days and three nights in the belly of a big fish, or a whale and remain alive. However, as indicated by a distinguished writer, James Bartley who was a sailor on a whaling ship in 1891 was swept overboard and was swallowed by a sperm whale which was harpooned and killed. But while the whale was being butchered the next day, (not three days and three nights like in Jonah's case), James Bartley's colleagues found him in the whale's stomach and rescued him.[11]

---

11 Mark D. Taylor, The Complete Book of Bible Literacy, Wheaton, Illinois: Tyndale House Publishers, 1992, p.162

How was Bartley able to survive in the whale's belly? He was not acting in disobedience like Jonah and never refused to go on a missionary journey for God, but he got thrown overboard the sailing ship. What can we attribute his being alive to? Definitely not luck, it has to be God using His Sovereign power, and in His mercy decided to spare Bartley's life. What should be noted is that, what is impossible for human beings is not impossible for God, (Luke 1:37; Mark 10:27).

> For with God nothing shall be impossible. Luke 1:37 AV

> And Jesus looking upon them saith, With men it is impossible, but not with God: for with God all things are possible. Mark 10:27 AV

Prayer Points

Father, I pray for (Mention the name if possible, ...), that he/she will stop walking in disobedience from now, and Lord, cause him/her to be restored in the name of Jesus Christ

Father, do the impossible in my life and family in the name of Jesus Christ

Father, do unusual miracles in my ministry in the name of Jesus Christ

Father, intervene in my business from today in the name of Jesus Christ

O Lord! be involved in all my entire journey in life in the name of Jesus Christ

Please take a moment to pray for all nations for forgiveness, mercy, healing and restoration in the name of Jesus Christ. God's Word says,

> If My people who are called by My name will humble themselves, and pray and seek My face, and turn from their wicked ways, then I will hear from heaven, and will forgive their sin and heal their land. 2 Chronicles 7:14

Through God's mercies Jonah was not abandoned, the Ninevites were spared the pending wrath and God's judgment, after they had fasted and prayed. But the universality of God's mercies becomes more obvious when one remembers how the one sent, (Jonah) and the city he was sent to, (Nineveh) were all forgiven and spared God's wrath and judgment. In spite of the critical views held by some school of thoughts, the story could not have been a myth or parable. We have read about the genealogy, the uniqueness of Jonah's call and commission, the special mercy which he received from God being unmatchable—all this should be evidential enough.

Believe it or not, as far as the Bible is concerned there was a miraculous provision for Jonah to get to Nineveh through a divine providence—a big fish was involved. Not only that, the question is, what do you make of the three days and three nights as Jesus remarked in the New Testament? This shall be the topic for our discussion in the next chapter.

CHAPTER EIGHT
THE THREE DAYS AND THREE NIGHTS

What Was Jonah's Book/Story Meant To Be?

The story about Jonah as being in the belly of a great fish for three days and three nights was deemed as a commentary, myth, history or parable, as some biblical critics want people to believe. However, one of the questions that comes to mind is, can a parable be so long as to contain four chapters as in the Book of Jonah? The truth is critics are entitled to their opinion, but what is undeniable is the universal power and mercy of God.[12] How did God show undeniable mercy in relation to the story in the Book of Jonah? There are five astounding ways God did that, and they can be deemed universal in nature too.

Five Undeniable Ways God Showed Mercy in Jonah's Book

1. God raised the storm but calmed it:

God used His power to raise the storm and calmed it at His will and this does not necessarily mean that the recipients of His mercy deserved it, (Jonah 1:4, 14-15).

> But the LORD sent out a great wind into the sea, and there was a mighty tempest in the sea, so that the ship was like to be broken. Jonah 1:4 AV

12 Derek Williams, (Ed.), New Concise Bible Dictionary, Leicester, England: Inter-Varsity Press, 1989, p. 283

Wherefore they cried unto the LORD, and said, We beseech thee, O LORD, we beseech thee, let us not perish for this man's life, and lay not upon us innocent blood: for thou, O LORD, hast done as it pleased thee. 15 So they took up Jonah, and cast him forth into the sea: and the sea ceased from her raging. Jonah 1:14-15 AV

2. Jonah was thrown into the sea but was not drowned:

Jonah was thrown into the sea, but God's power and mercy showed up and the great fish which was already prepared and waiting there, took Jonah (who was given a second chance to live) to the beach of the sea at the Assyrian capital and vomited him out, (Jonah 2:10).

And the LORD spake unto the fish, and it vomited out Jonah upon the dry land. Jonah 2:10 AV

3. God's unusual mercy was extended to the mariners:

God's unusual mercy and power touched the lives of the sailors and their co-travellers (likely to be Phoenicians), and were spared even though we are not told directly about their nationalities except Jonah who was an Hebrew, (Jonah 1:13-16).

Nevertheless the men rowed hard to bring it to the land; but they could not: for the sea wrought, and was tempestuous against them. 14 Wherefore they cried unto the LORD, and said, We beseech thee, O LORD, we beseech thee, let us not perish for this man's life, and lay not upon us innocent blood: for thou, O LORD, hast done as it pleased thee. 15 So they took up Jonah, and cast him forth into the sea: and the sea ceased from her raging. 16 Then the men feared the LORD exceedingly, and offered a sacrifice unto the LORD, and made vows. Jonah 1:13-16 AV

4. God withheld His judgement towards the Ninevites:

Not just humans as shown above, but also their herd and flock (beast) had to fast and wear sackcloth, (Jonah 3:7-8). As it turned out, they were spared from God's judgment because of the mercy of God.

> And he caused it to be proclaimed and published through Nineveh by the decree of the king and his nobles, saying, Let neither man nor beast, herd nor flock, taste any thing: let them not feed, nor drink water: 8 but let man and beast be covered with sackcloth, and cry mightily unto God: yea, let them turn every one from his evil way, and from the violence that is in their hands. Jonah 3:7-8 AV

5. God's love and mercies are meant to extend to other parts of the world:

The sending of the prophet from Israel to the Assyrian capital is an indication that God's love and mercy should be allowed to extend to other parts of the world, read again as in below (Jonah 3:7-10). In a nutshell, Jonah's missional journey to Nineveh is meant to be a testament that, God's love, mercy, and salvation were never meant to be confined to Israel alone, (Romans 3:29).

> 7 And he caused it to be proclaimed and published through Nineveh by the decree of the king and his nobles, saying, Let neither man nor beast, herd nor flock, taste any thing: let them not feed, nor drink water: 8 but let man and beast be covered with

sackcloth, and cry mightily unto God: yea, let them turn every one from his evil way, and from the violence that is in their hands. 9 Who can tell if God will turn and repent, and turn away from his fierce anger, that we perish not? 10 And God saw their works, that they turned from their evil way; and God repented of the evil, that he had said that he would do unto them; and he did it not. Jonah 3:7-10 AV

Is he the God of the Jews only? is he not also of the Gentiles? Yes, of the Gentiles also: Romans 3:29 AV

Jesus Alludes To Himself

It is significant to note that, the allusion to three days and three nights as Jesus mentioned in (Matthew 12:40), was parallel to that of Jonah who was in the belly of the big fish for the same number of days.

For as Jonas was three days and three nights in the whale's belly; so shall the Son of man be three days and three nights in the heart of the earth. Matthew 12:40 AV

But most importantly, the above biblical comment was meant to draw attention to the three days of Jesus' own death, burial and resurrection. In other words, the reference to Jonah's experience prefigured the Lord's passion and resurrection.[13] Put simply, Jesus was alluding to Himself when that comment was made.

---

13 William MacDonald, Art Farstad (Ed.), Believer's Bible Commentary - A Complete Bible Commentary in One Volume, London: Thomas Nelson Publishers, 1995, p. 1252

Non-believers Can Receive God's Compassion

Again, in regards to the allusion to the three days and three nights, what should be a concern is that, while the Ninevites heeded the warning and repented, would Jesus' audience willingly and genuinely be ready to repent in their current climate after His resurrection? Are things better, or closer to (Luke 11:29-32), where it was predicted that nations would be at war with each other, that lawfulness and love for God would decrease?

> And when the people were gathered thick together, he began to say, This is an evil generation: they seek a sign; and there shall no sign be given it, but the sign of Jonas the prophet. 30 For as Jonas was a sign unto the Ninevites, so shall also the Son of man be to this generation. 31 The queen of the south shall rise up in the judgment with the men of this generation, and condemn them: for she came from the utmost parts of the earth to hear the wisdom of Solomon; and, behold, a greater than Solomon is here. 32 The men of Nineveh shall rise up in the judgment with this generation, and shall condemn it: for they repented at the preaching of Jonas; and, behold, a greater than Jonas is here. Luke 11:29-32

Thus far, it is absolutely clear that, the book of Jonah does not suggest universalism about all people or nations being chosen, but does teach that non-believing peoples may still benefit in some ways from God's compassion.[14]

---

14 Douglas Stuart, Contribution on the Book of Jonah in New Bible Commentary, 21st Century Edition, Leicester, England: Inter-Varsity Press, 1994, p. 814

Proponents Of Mercy And Compassion

Although a prophet of Yahweh, yet Jonah seems not to have a jot of compassion in his heart for the Assyrians who were sworn enemies of Israel. In any case, there is need to behave like how Jesus would behave if He were here now, or at least try and learn. What?

It is imperative to show mercy and be compassionate to one another—we can learn from Jonah's book and change for the better. As far as God is concerned, whether we like it or not, salvation should be preferred to destruction of any soul in towns, cities, and in all the nations of this world put together. This is what God desires for us.

Finally, the way and manner in which God dealt with the situation at Nineveh by practically involving Jonah when He used the plant or gourd, is a great lesson for today's Christian believers. If God can use a plant or gourd to help Jonah understand what it meant to show mercy and compassion to any person, definitely God is saying, we must be proponents of mercy and compassion from now onwards. Also, it means we all have to be merciful and compassionate to anyone who repents genuinely, (Jonah 4:9-11).

> And God said to Jonah, Doest thou well to be angry for the gourd? And he said, I do well to be angry, even unto death. 10 Then said the LORD, Thou hast had pity on the gourd, for the which thou hast not laboured, neither madest it grow; which came up in a night, and perished in a night: 11 and should not I spare Nineveh, that great city, wherein are more than sixscore thousand persons that cannot discern between their right hand and their left hand; and also much cattle?
> Jonah 4:9-11 AV

Have you been traumatised before, or do you know someone who had some traumatic experience in the past or recently? I am obligated to say that the book of Jonah in one of its themes demonstrates how people most likely had some traumatic or panic experience, but God helped them out.

Looking Back On

Cast your mind back to where the storm started to rage against the mariners and their passengers, think about the point where it was agreed that Jonah should be thrown into the sea, consider when the news about the impending doom at Nineveh was delivered to the king and his reaction, and finally the entire city—the people and their families and businesses and so on. What could your imaginations be like? Definitely not a laughable matter. In this present era, the effects of artificial intelligence (AI) and the social media, their influencers, theorists and propagandists would have spread the news about the Ninevites the way it suited them. No one would have been able to rule out divisive opinions.

But the undeniable fact remains that, the mercies of God prevailed over the judgment. We must be proponents of mercy and compassion, frankly, act as if Jesus is physically present and waiting to see you show mercy and compassion to your neighbour.

To conclude, it should be remembered that, Jesus' reference to Jonah's experience about the three days and three nights in the belly of the big fish, prefigured His (Jesus) passion and resurrection, that is, He drew attention to His own death, burial and resurrection. That being the case, we all have to become advocates of God's mercies wherever we find ourselves, because the redemption that Jesus provided us, through the Cross, must not be taken for granted. However, like Jonah, do we really know the depth of the mercies of God for humanity? Do we care to know about it? We shall see what the discussion holds for us in the next chapter.

CHAPTER NINE
GOD'S MERCY WAS GREATER THAN WHAT JONAH KNEW

Was Jonah Traumatised?

When discussing about the nature of the mercies of God towards Jonah, it should be realised that people go through seasons in life, and we should not expect God to respond emotionally the way humans do. Humans are temperamental, can be forgetful and there's a limit to what we know, and can endure. Further, humans are prone to errors, limitations and weaknesses. Furthermore, on many occasions people can be seen as weak, gullible, feeble, fragile and vulnerable. God is never like that. That is why we can never realise the extent of His mercy towards us, Jonah included.

But note that, Jonah had his own share of tragedy during the near-shipwreck. Was it not possible for him to think God wouldn't be merciful to him? That the end of his life had come? Was it not possible for him to be traumatised after the incident? Imagine if he was caught unprepared in the entire incident? Yet, reflecting over the entire incident we know that God's mercy was greater than Jonah knew or thought.

Did God Concede Too Much To Jonah?

God's approach in handling the situation was totally different. It makes one think that He (God) was condoning and conceding too much to Jonah. How? That is, by allowing the runaway evangelist to indulge in his prejudices and rebellion. As if to suggest to God, "Why not dump Jonah and use someone else?" However, whatever the opinion you hold, it is worth remembering that God keeps His promises and covenant, and He weighs all His actions before doing any thing. Most importantly, He is beyond all human errors, vulnerabilities and limitations. Therefore, God did not concede too much, rather He was keeping His covenant with the patriarchs in view.

God Is A Covenant Keeper

We recall that Jonah was an Israelite who comes under the Abrahamic covenant and historically, God had an established covenant with the Israelites since the time of Abraham, and Jonah was one of the great grand children of Abraham. The following Bible passages form part of the essential fundamental references, (Genesis 12:1-2a; 15:4-5; 17:6-8; 18:16-17; 22:3-5, 15-18).

> Now the LORD had said to Abram: "Get out of your country, From your family And from your father's house, To a land that I will show you. 2 I will make you a great nation; Genesis 12:1-2a

> And behold, the word of the LORD came to him, saying, "This one shall not be your heir, but one who will come from your own body shall be your heir." 5 Then He brought him outside and said, "Look now toward heaven, and count the stars if you are able to number them." And He said to him, "So shall your descendants be." Genesis 15:4-5

> I will make you exceedingly fruitful; and I will make nations of you, and kings shall come from you. 7 And I will establish My covenant between Me and you and your descendants after you in their generations, for an

103

everlasting covenant, to be God to you and your descendants after you. 8 Also I give to you and your descendants after you the land in which you are a stranger, all the land of Canaan, as an everlasting possession; and I will be their God." Genesis 17:6-8

Then the men rose from there and looked toward Sodom, and Abraham went with them to send them on the way. 17 And the LORD said, "Shall I hide from Abraham what I am doing, 18 since Abraham shall surely become a great and mighty nation, and all the nations of the earth shall be blessed in him? Genesis 18:16-18

So Abraham rose early in the morning and saddled his donkey, and took two of his young men with him, and Isaac his son; and he split the wood for the burnt offering, and arose and went to the place of which God had told him. 4 Then on the third day Abraham lifted his eyes and saw the place afar off. 5 And Abraham said to his young men, "Stay here with the donkey; the lad and I will go yonder and worship, and we will come back to you," ... 15 Then the Angel of the LORD called to Abraham a second time out of heaven, 16 and said: "By Myself I have sworn, says the LORD, because you have done this thing, and have not withheld your son, your only son—17 blessing I will bless you, and multiplying I will multiply your descendants as the stars of the heaven and as the sand which is on the seashore; and your descendants shall possess the gate of their enemies. 18 In your seed all the nations of the earth shall be blessed, because you have obeyed My voice." Genesis 22:3-5, 15-18

By way of analogy, Jonah who is the main character in this book comes from the tribe of Zebulun and he was the sixth son of Jacob. I have given an elaborate explanation in one of the sections in this book (Chapter One), subtitled, The Genealogy of Jonah. Furthermore, it must be noted that the family tree of Jacob/Israel started from the relationship between God and Abraham.

Abraham As God's Channel To Others

Firstly, the people who came out of Abraham lineage are meant to be custodians of God's law. Secondly, they are meant to be stewards of the prophecies of the Messiah to come. In particular, the Messiah was being referred to, in (Genesis 22:18a), as the "Seed" or "Offspring." We should not be surprised that apostle Paul supported this argument in (Galatians 3:16).

> Now to Abraham and his Seed were the promises made. He does not say, "And to seeds," as of many, but as of one, "And to your Seed," who is Christ. Galatians 3:16

Importantly, the patriarch, (Abraham) should be seen as God's channel, or the family tree through whom the ancestral link would be connected to the coming Messiah, who is Jesus Christ. That through Him, all the people in the world would receive eternal life—this is in the context of (Genesis 22:18a) stating, "in your seed all the nations of the earth shall be blessed." In a nutshell, Jesus is an offspring of Abraham, but also the Messiah or Christ, as declared in (Luke 1:30-33). It is a universal programme and is not based on Nineveh alone.

> Then the angel said to her, "Do not be afraid, Mary, for you have found favor with God. 31 And behold, you will conceive in your womb and bring forth a Son, and shall call His name JESUS. 32 He will be great, and will

be called the Son of the Highest; and the Lord God will give Him the throne of His father David. 33 And He will reign over the house of Jacob forever, and of His kingdom there will be no end." Luke 1:30-33

Isaac, The Promised Heir With Archetypical Symbols Of Christ

Of course, Isaac was the promised heir and not the "seed," as we noted in (Genesis 22:18). Who was he then? There are two ways to consider the archetypical symbols of Christ in that regard. First of all, Isaac was an archetype or a model of Christ by being the only son and loved by his father (Abraham), and willing to do his father's will like Jesus did to His Father. Genuinely, Abraham was ready to offer Isaac to God, as expressed in (Genesis 22:9-13). Let us read,

> Then they came to the place of which God had told him. And Abraham built an altar there and placed the wood in order; and he bound Isaac his son and laid him on the altar, upon the wood. 10 And Abraham stretched out his hand and took the knife to slay his son. 11 But the Angel of the LORD called to him from heaven and said, "Abraham, Abraham!" So he said, "Here I am." 12 And He said, "Do not lay your hand on the lad, or do anything to him; for now I know that you fear God, since you have not withheld your son, your only son, from Me." 13 Then Abraham lifted his eyes and looked, and there behind him was a ram caught in a thicket by its horns. So Abraham went and took the ram, and offered it up for a burnt offering instead of his son. Genesis 22:9-13

Secondly, the ram which was caught in a thicket by its horns served as an innocent substitute, its blood was shed, it died and was offered to God as a burnt offering on Mount

Moriah.[15] It is worth remembering that Jesus remains the innocent Substitute which God provided for Himself for the redemption of humanity, although He (Jesus) was crucified, killed, hanged on the Cross at Calvary, (a vicarious penalty for our sins), but He rose again on the third day, hallelujah!

Another crucial statement which must be made relates to Israel being described as a chosen nation. Why was this so? This "chosenness" must be understood from the standpoint of one man through whom God brought out a nation by the patriarch's (Abraham) grandson called Jacob who was one of the twin sons of Isaac. To recall, genealogically, the Messiah came out of this lineage. More on this shortly, but suffice to say that God is a Promise-keeper. And as a result of His covenant, God had to treat the Israelites of the Old Testament differently from the other nations and their people. Were it possible, especially as humans, people wouldn't hesitate to say God was discriminatory towards other nations on this earth.

However, the all-wise and all-knowing God will not do a thing without a reason. He chose the nation of Israel (a microcosmic group, that is a model), over other nations to be a show-piece for humanity, especially, for emulation in regards to the relationship He intended for Himself ahead of today, so that all peoples on earth can be blessed, (Genesis 12:3).

> I will bless those who bless you, And I will curse him who curses you; And in you all the families of the earth shall be blessed." Genesis 12:3

Additionally, God's intention has been to keep the Israelites as His special treasure above all people, and for them to be a kingdom of priests and a holy nation to Him. In return, the

---

15   William MacDonld, (Art Farstad, ed.), Believer's Bible Commentary, London: Thomas Nelson Publishers, 1989, p. 59

Israelites have to obey God and keep His commandments, as narrated in (Exodus 19:3-6). Whether God's intention has been achieved or not, is left for a future research.

> And Moses went up to God, and the LORD called to him from the mountain, saying, "Thus you shall say to the house of Jacob, and tell the children of Israel: 4 'You have seen what I did to the Egyptians, and how I bore you on eagles' wings and brought you to Myself. 5 Now therefore, if you will indeed obey My voice and keep My covenant, then you shall be a special treasure to Me above all people; for all the earth is Mine. 6 And you shall be to Me a kingdom of priests and a holy nation.' These are the words which you shall speak to the children of Israel." Exodus 19:3-6

Kindness Or Grace From God

In spite of the above observations, one of the careful consideration for this moment is to ask ourselves how much of God's mercies Jonah knew about. The type of mercy which was shown to Jonah is (*chesed*, in Hebrew). It means kindness or grace which emanates from God, see below, (Figure 1). Would God of all flesh show kindness or grace despite the noted shortcomings from Jonah? We shall see.

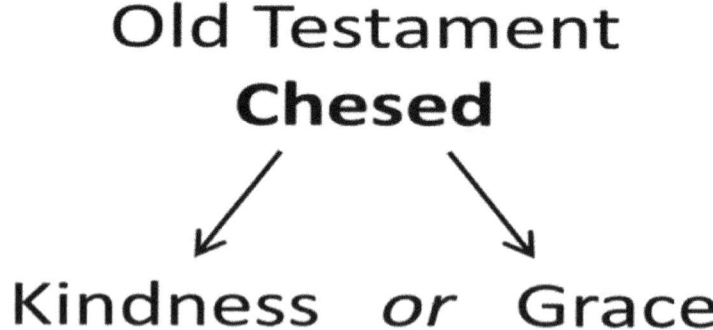

Figure 1

Obviously, what Jonah required after going the opposite direction was beyond ordinary help, it was abundant mercy which solely depended on God's benevolence, not on merit—that is, *chesed*. In this context, it refers to God who in His faithfulness treated His people mercifully. He (God) was not indebted or compelled to do so, but He chose to. Thus like Jonah, any of us really need God's help at any time. May God be gracious to you. To buttress this point, on one occasion God said to Moses when He had a dialogue with him, refer to (Exodus 33:19b).

> I will be gracious to whom I will be gracious, and I will have compassion on whom I will have compassion. Exodus 33:19b

It should be appreciated that God chose from time immemorial to graciously act in a particular manner, that is, to keep to His established covenant which He made with the Old Testament patriarchs. First, with Abraham, and Isaac, then Jacob—out of whom came the twelve tribes of Israel. Take for instance, what was said in (Genesis 12:1-7; and 17:1-7). Let us read,

> Now the LORD had said to Abram: "Get out of your country, From your family And from your father's house, To a land that I will show you. 2 I will make you a great nation; I will bless you And make your name great; And you shall be a blessing. 3 I will bless those who bless you, And I will curse him who curses you; And in you all the families of the earth shall be blessed." 4 So Abram departed as the LORD had spoken to him, and Lot went with him. Abram was seventy-five years old when he departed from Haran. 5 Then Abram took Sarai his wife and Lot his brother's son, and all their possessions that they had gathered, and the people

whom they had acquired in Haran, and they departed to go to the land of Canaan. So they came to the land of Canaan. 6 Abram passed through the land to the place of Shechem, as far as the terebinth tree of Moreh. And the Canaanites were then in the land. 7 Then the LORD appeared to Abram and said, "To your descendants I will give this land." And there he built an altar to the LORD, who had appeared to him. Genesis 12:1-7

When Abram was ninety-nine years old, the LORD appeared to Abram and said to him, "I am Almighty God; walk before Me and be blameless. 2 And I will make My covenant between Me and you, and will multiply you exceedingly." 3 Then Abram fell on his face, and God talked with him, saying: 4 "As for Me, behold, My covenant is with you, and you shall be a father of many nations. 5 No longer shall your name be called Abram, but your name shall be Abraham; for I have made you a father of many nations. 6 I will make you exceedingly fruitful; and I will make nations of you, and kings shall come from you. 7 And I will establish My covenant between Me and you and your descendants after you in their generations, for an everlasting covenant, to be God to you and your descendants after you. Genesis 17:1-7

Incomprehensible Mercy

What makes the above promises which God gave to the patriarch to be described as inexplicable or incomprehensible mercy is, because it was instigated by God's kindness or grace (*chesed*). This type of 'mercy' motivated by God's kindness or grace was shown to Jonah, were it not so, his life would not have been spared. Did Jonah ever knew that?

I pray that every type of mercy that would benefit you, your family, and your generation be granted in the name of Jesus Christ.

Further, it must be emphasised that God graciously chose to keep His established covenant and acted mercifully, because left for the Israelites although they were covenanted people, they would never have earned or qualified for it, no matter how hard they try to. Let us consider a reading from (Psalm 89:27-28).

> Also I will make him My firstborn, The highest of the kings of the earth. 28 My mercy I will keep for him forever, And My covenant shall stand firm with him. Psalm 89:27-28

Be it known in the above cited text that, God took seriously His divine promise with David who was a type of Christ, and amazingly His succession plan in relation to the Saviour who was to be born many years later, we can refer to (Matthew 1:2-6, 16-17) for confirmation.

> Abraham begot Isaac, Isaac begot Jacob, and Jacob begot Judah and his brothers. 3 Judah begot Perez and Zerah by Tamar, Perez begot Hezron, and Hezron begot Ram. 4 Ram begot Amminadab, Amminadab begot Nahshon, and Nahshon begot Salmon. 5 Salmon begot Boaz by Rahab, Boaz begot Obed by Ruth, Obed begot Jesse, 6 and Jesse begot David the king. David the king begot Solomon by her who had been the wife of Uriah ...

> And Jacob begot Joseph the husband of Mary, of whom was born Jesus who is called Christ. 17 So all the generations from Abraham to David are fourteen generations, from David until the captivity in Babylon

are fourteen generations, and from the captivity in Babylon until the Christ are fourteen generations. Matthew 1:2-6, 16-17

There is no individual that can earn this type of highest honour and a merciful act from God through their hard-work, except it was conferred on the person like God did to David. To cap it all, God said, "My covenant shall stand firm with him." The type of mercy which led to this pronouncement is undoubtedly extraordinary. Simply, the above statement relates to God's loving-kindness (*chesed*) and faithfulness,[16] out of which came the mercies shown. No power on earth could have had the capacity or capability to wrestle, negotiate successfully, or snatch this type of divine promise (deal or bargain?) from God. Never!

In this vein, we can see how in a typical way, God who chose graciously to act in an exceptional manner to keep His established covenant which He gracefully made with the Old Testament patriarchs, did not find it difficult to do it again in Jonah's life when the need arose. He (God) showed mercy to Jonah who hails from the lineage of Zebulun, the son of Jacob, Jacob the son of Isaac, and Isaac the son of Abraham, and Abraham, the friend of God, (James 2:23).

> And the Scripture was fulfilled which says, "Abraham believed God, and it was accounted to him for righteousness." And he was called the friend of God. James 2:23

It was this same God that came to Jonah's rescue the moment he was thrown into the stormy sea—for God had already

---

16 Kyle M. Yates, Writing on The Book of Psalms in Charles F. Pfeiffer, (Ed.,), The Wycliffe Bible Commentary, Chicago: Moody Press, 1962, p. 528

prepared a great fish to swallow Jonah and it carried him to safety, (Jonah 1:17). Not only that, God preserved Jonah's life and made it possible for him to carry out his ministerial task at Nineveh. The Lord will preserve you and you will fulfil your destiny.

Definitely, Yahweh, the God of Israel, had the option to turn His face away, or to the other side because of Jonah's rebellious and insensitive attitude, but He (God) didn't, which again, can be attributed to Him as being merciful to Jonah, mercy which was impelled by His kindness or grace (*chesed*). This is what I describe as, "Mercy beyond what Jonah knew". Some critics might not really appreciate the magnitude of God's mercies that Jonah received, unless they understand the nature of his commission. In destiny, the Lord will not replace you with another person, amen.

Prayer Points

God who went all the way with Jonah, have mercy on me, and be with me throughout my lifetime, in the name of Jesus Christ

God who went all the way with Jonah, have mercy on me and let me fulfil my destiny in the name of Jesus Christ

God who went all the way with Jonah, have mercy on me and don't allow my destiny to be aborted in the name of Jesus Christ

God who showed abundant mercies to Jonah, fill my entire life with your plentiful mercies in the name of Jesus Christ

No matter the storm in life, God who stood by Jonah, stand by me

— Stand by my family
— Stand by my ministry
— Stand by my business, in the name of Jesus Christ, amen.

Give God praise and thanks for answering your prayers.

Believe it or not, Jonah had his encounter, had his share of God's kindness or grace, (Hebrew:*chesed*), and at the end of the four chapters of his book, God's purpose was achieved. It is left for us to learn as much as we can, and trust God to extend His immeasurable mercies to us. Indeed, there is no end to what we can learn from Jonah's book. To further deepen our knowledge, we can compare Jonah with two biblical characters namely, Pharaoh and Job in the next chapter to acquire some wisdom from their encounters with God.

Chapter Ten
A GLANCE AT JONAH, PHARAOH AND JOB

Intentionality

God will never do a thing without a purpose. Most importantly, all His actions carry eternal intentions and consequences—good or bad it might seem to us. That being said, we should put all guesswork or bias aside. He dealt with Pharaoh as we know for a purpose, some of which are stated below. In the same vein, when it was time to deal with Jonah, God was able to teach him to be compassionate and non-judgemental.

However, as we shall be reading about Job shortly, one begins to wonder, what did he do to deserve the crisis he had to suffer? Definitely, God had His purpose for that, yet I have heard people ask, "Why do bad things happen to good people?." Perhaps you have gone through some tragedy, or are going through, realise that God has His purpose in what is happening to you. Acting as if an undercover news reporter, let us consider Pharaoh's story to be followed by Job's, but periodically, we shall discuss more about Jonah.

Stubborn Pharaoh—Who To Blame?

The Pharaoh being referred to here is Ramesses II. He was the Pharaoh during the time of Exodus in the Bible. The records stated that, he embarked on great and ambitious building projects and was the one who purportedly built the famous East-delta residence of Pi-Ramesse, read (Exodus 5:1-7).

> Afterward Moses and Aaron went in and told Pharaoh, "Thus says the LORD God of Israel: 'Let My people go, that they may hold a feast to Me in the wilderness.' " 2 And Pharaoh said "Who is the Lord, that I should obey His voice to let Israel go? I do not know the Lord, nor will I let Israel go? " 3 So they said, "The God of the Hebrews has met with us. Please, let us go three days' journey into the desert and sacrifice to the LORD our God, lest He fall upon us with pestilence or with the sword." 4 Then the king of Egypt said to them, "Moses and Aaron, why do you take the people from their work? Get back to your labor." 5 And Pharaoh said, "Look, the people of the land are many now, and you make them rest from their labor!" 6 So the same day Pharaoh commanded the taskmasters of the people and their officers, saying, 7 "You shall no longer give the people straw to make brick as before. Let them go and gather straw for themselves. Exodus 5:1-7

Some historian documents about this Pharaoh had striking resemblance with the story in (Exodus 5:1-7) above. The documents narrated how he (Pharaoh) ordered men to cut and drag stones, and stated his unwillingness to allow the Hebrews to go on public holidays, (referring to the time when Moses requested that they be allowed three days to go and offer a sacrifice to God, see (Exodus 5:2-3). In addition, his refusal to recognise Moses' God, and the eventual hot pursuit is expressed in (Exodus 14:7).[17]

---

17 K. A Kitchen, Writing on Egypt in David and Pat Alexander, The Lion Handbook to the Bible, Oxford, England: Lion Publishing plc, 1983, pp. 153-154

So he made ready his chariot and took his people with him. 7 Also, he took six hundred choice chariots, and all the chariots of Egypt with captains over every one of them. Exodus 14:6-7

There's A Reason For Whatever God Does

Interestingly, there could be instances where God was acting behind the scene in regards to some incidents that took place in one's life without you knowing it. From the above narration, Pharaoh terribly and mercilessly dealt with the Israelites, but once God's purpose was achieved, He permitted the Israelites to depart from Egypt. But, it should not be surprising that God was behind Pharaoh's stubbornness, read (Exodus 4:21).

And the LORD said to Moses, "When you go back to Egypt, see that you do all those wonders before Pharaoh which I have put in your hand. But I will harden his heart, so that he will not let the people go. Exodus 4:21

Who would have thought that God could do that? Nevertheless, understand that He had his reason for doing so. We need to prayerfully search our hearts from time to time when things happen, and not jump into conclusion swiftly, because God might have a different intention that could be unknown to us. Further, we need to prayerfully entreat the Lord and once we are sure about what is happening, then begin a spiritual warfare.

Some other things we could do include, when going through challenges one can prayerfully ask God for strength, endurance, and the wisdom required to handle the situation. Also, do not fail to ask for the revelation about His purpose for the crisis, while at the same time, entreating or asking for

His will to be done. Remember, Jesus once asked God, "Can this cup pass over me?" and He remarked immediately, "Not my will" as expressed in (Matthew 26:42-44). Let us read,

> Again, a second time, He went away and prayed, saying, "O My Father, if this cup cannot pass away from Me unless I drink it, Your will be done." 43 And He came and found them asleep again, for their eyes were heavy. 44 So He left them, went away again, and prayed the third time, saying the same words. Matthew 26:42-44

God who heard the cry and sorrows of the Israelites at some stage, was ready to take them out of the affliction to a land flowing with milk and honey, according to (Exodus 3:17). But, that was not the only occasion God acted behind the scene, we remember that He acted again when He sent locusts (the eighth plague), to cover the surface of the entire nation of Egypt, see (Exodus 10:1-2), let us read,

> Now the LORD said to Moses, "Go in to Pharaoh; for I have hardened his heart and the hearts of his servants, that I may show these signs of Mine before him, 2 and that you may tell in the hearing of your son and your son's son the mighty things I have done in Egypt, and My signs which I have done among them, that you may know that I am the LORD." Exodus 10:1-2

God will never do a thing without a reason, therefore, for His purpose to come to pass, He went on till the tenth plague was unleashed. Why did He do that? God did that to establish an enduring legacy of His mighty power and sovereignty. Another intention was that, while individuals might be dazed by the experience, let the knowledge of the event be permanent with us, but outlive us to the degree that the lesson learned, is passed on to benefit our children and to many others. More so, to our future generations. By so doing, the future generation will be able to learn to esteem and serve God with fear and trembling. To you my reader, even when the opportunity for repentance looks slim, we are to encourage sinners to repent so that they (sinners) will not have excuse when judgment is eventually served. As we know, Pharaoh was judged at some point in (Exodus 14:28),

> Then the waters returned and covered the chariots, the horsemen, and all the army of Pharaoh that came into the sea after them. Not so much as one of them remained. Exodus 14:28

Remember that the same God who was behind the storm that nearly took Jonah's life, was the same God who was behind Pharaoh's heart which was hardened. Notice also that, while Jonah was spared, Pharaoh Ramesses II was not spared, the only reason is because God's mercy was not extended to him. May God's mercy extend to you, rest and abide with you in the name of Jesus Christ. On another occasion which would be the last opportunity for Ramesses II, God had His purpose for acting again, but it was behind the scene. The venue was to be the approach to the Red Sea. When the moment came, Pharaoh had intended to capture his 'runaway slaves' (the Israelites) back to Egypt and he expressed his desire as recorded in (Exodus 15:9). Let us read,

> I will pursue, I will overtake, I will divide the spoil; My desire shall be satisfied on them. I will draw my sword, My hand shall destroy them. Exodus 15:9

However, the God of the Hebrews that he (Pharaoh Ramesses II) disrespected and disobeyed, dealt ruthlessly with him according to (Exodus 15:10),

You blew with Your wind, The sea covered them; They sank like lead in the mighty waters.

Notwithstanding, God's purpose was to gain glory and honour over that Pharaoh, the power of Egypt, their gods and their armies which were the strongest and most powerful during that time. As you can see, the earthly king had his purpose for the challenge and pursuit of the Israelites. But on the other hand, God, the King of kings, the God of the armies of Israel had His purpose too. When the two powers collided, the lesser power terminated—Pharaoh, his army, chariots and horsemen perished in the Red Sea, we serve a mighty God! Let us read (Exodus 14:27),

And Moses stretched out his hand over the sea; and when the morning appeared, the sea returned to its full depth, while the Egyptians were fleeing into it. So the LORD overthrew the Egyptians in the midst of the sea. Exodus 14:27

May every 'Pharaoh' in your life be eliminated in the name of Jesus Christ. Pharaoh represented pain, enslavement, hard labour, torment, lack of peace and so on, in the lives of the Israelites during that time. My prayer for you is that, you shall no longer see the Pharaohs in your life in the name of Jesus Christ. Apart from Jonah and Pharaoh as explained earlier, another person that comes to mind is Job who lost all his wealth, his beautiful children, and suffered ill health, but unbelievably he continued to serve God. Who could this Job be?

The Man Called Job—A non-Israelite

It seems Jonah deserves to suffer some punishments for his actions but not Job, especially, if we read our Bible very well. The biblical account states that Job was a righteous and

God-fearing person who lived in a geographical area called the land of Uz. There are two biblical references to this effect, (Job 1:1), and (Lamentations 4:21a).

> There was a man in the land of Uz, whose name was Job; and that man was blameless and upright, and one who feared God and shunned evil, Job 1:1.

What a description! As stated above, he was a man who lived in the land of Uz which is Edom, in south-east of Palestine and that location has equally been confirmed in (Lamentation 4:21a) which reads,

> Rejoice and be glad, O daughter of Edom, You who dwell in the land of Uz! Lamentation 4:21a

While Jonah deserved to be punished on the account of what we read about his disobedience, in the end God's ultimate aim which is the most important was achieved. But why should Job be allowed to suffer terrible losses for no sin?

Interestingly, apart from the geographical location as presented to us, what is more surprising is that, unlike other patriarchs, Job was a non-Israelite. Further, he is described as a worshipper and calls his God—Elohim that is, a true God, the same God the Israelites call Yahweh, the personal name of God.[18] But, it is much more fascinating to see the way God described this man (Job) on a particular day. God referred to him as "my servant" in (Job 1:8). Let us read,

> Then the LORD said to Satan, "Have you considered My servant Job, that there is none like him on the

---

18 David J. A. Clines, Writing on Job in D. A. Carson, et al, (Consulting Editor), New Bible Commentary 21st Century Edition, Leicester, England: Inter-Varsity Press, 1994, p. 463

earth, a blameless and upright man, one who fears God and shuns evil?" Job 1:8

The Theme of "My Servant"

Whoever God calls "my servant" is not an ordinary person. If you watch carefully, it would be discovered that, such individuals have special peculiarity, and always distinguish themselves in the area of their calling or assignment. They don't disappoint God no matter the challenge, God knows that. The above two words "my servant" catch our attention in that God called a non-Israelite "my servant".

This reference identifies by description with the likes of Moses and David to mention this two, whom we know were distinguished individuals in their calling, the tasks they undertook according to their commission, and how they walked with God as Israelites. It is not about trying to put them together on an equal pedestal, or do a comparative analysis on them. But rather, it is important to note that the reference, "my servant", was meant to grant recognition and denote the significance that God Himself bestowed on such individuals and their performance. Was there any time their individual tasks were easy? I do not think so.

"My Servant"—The Mosaic Example

A little survey about the patriarchs or those who were called "my servant", would show that the challenges they faced individually, their assignment and how they responded during their respective tasks were non-equivalent. For instance, Moses we remember was the leader of God's people from Egypt. He was called and commissioned to lead them from bondage, as recorded in (Exodus 3:10; 12:50-51). The task was not easy whichever way it is considered.

> Come now, therefore, and I will send you to Pharaoh that you may bring My people, the children of Israel, out of Egypt. Exodus 3:10

> Thus all the children of Israel did; as the LORD commanded Moses and Aaron, so they did. 51 And it came to pass, on that very same day, that the LORD brought the children of Israel out of the land of Egypt according to their armies. Exodus 12:50-51

Regardless of our views, with God's help Moses led them to the periphery of the Promised Land, precisely the land of Moab and he died on Mount Nebo, as stated in (Deuteronomy 32:48-50; 34:1-5).

> Then the LORD spoke to Moses that very same day, saying: 49 "Go up this mountain of the Abarim, Mount Nebo, which is in the land of Moab, across from Jericho; view the land of Canaan, which I give to the children of Israel as a possession; 50 and die on the mountain which you ascend, and be gathered to your people, just as Aaron your brother died on Mount Hor and was gathered to his people. Deuteronomy 32:48-50

> Then Moses went up from the plains of Moab to Mount Nebo, to the top of Pisgah, which is across from Jericho. And the LORD showed him all the land of Gilead as far as Dan, 2 all Naphtali and the land of Ephraim and Manasseh, all the land of Judah as far as the Western Sea, 3 the South, and the plain of the Valley of Jericho, the city of palm trees, as far as Zoar. 4 Then the LORD said to him, "This is the land of which

I swore to give Abraham, Isaac, and Jacob, saying, 'I will give it to your descendants.' I have caused you to see it with your eyes, but you shall not cross over there." 5 So Moses the servant of the LORD died there in the land of Moab, according to the word of the LORD. Deuteronomy 34:1-5

Nonetheless, prior to his death, some other significant instances where God referred to Moses as "my servant" include, (Numbers 12:8; Joshua 1:2), and (Malachi 4:4).

I speak with him face to face, Even plainly, and not in dark sayings; And he sees the form of the LORD. Why then were you not afraid To speak against My servant Moses?" Numbers 12:8

"Moses My servant is dead. Now therefore, arise, go over this Jordan, you and all this people, to the land which I am giving to them—the children of Israel. Joshua 1:2

"Remember the Law of Moses, My servant, Which I commanded him in Horeb for all Israel, With the statutes and judgments. Malachi 4:4

After the theme of "my servant" as shown in the above two examples, that is, for Job and Moses, our attention will now be turned to David.

Davidic Example

David, a shepherd and warrior was the individual who killed Goliath as recorded in (1 Samuel 17:48-51),

So it was, when the Philistine arose and came and drew near to meet David, that David hurried and ran toward the army to meet the Philistine. 49 Then David put his

124

hand in his bag and took out a stone; and he slung it and struck the Philistine in his forehead, so that the stone sank into his forehead, and he fell on his face to the earth. 50 So David prevailed over the Philistine with a sling and a stone, and struck the Philistine and killed him. But there was no sword in the hand of David. 51 Therefore David ran and stood over the Philistine, took his sword and drew it out of its sheath and killed him, and cut off his head with it. And when the Philistines saw that their champion was dead, they fled. 1 Samuel 17:48-51

Further, David became a king who first reigned in Hebron, see (2 Samuel 2:11),

And the time that David was king in Hebron over the house of Judah was seven years and six months. 2 Samuel 2:11

Again, he was anointed as king over Israel, as recorded in (2 Samuel 5:2-4),

Also, in time past, when Saul was king over us, you were the one who led Israel out and brought them in; and the LORD said to you, 'You shall shepherd My people Israel, and be ruler over Israel.' " 3 Therefore all the elders of Israel came to the king at Hebron, and King David made a covenant with them at Hebron before the LORD. And they anointed David king over Israel. 4 David was thirty years old when he began to reign, and he reigned forty years. 2 Samuel 5:2-4

David fought numerous battles and won with God's help. As we celebrate the achievements of Moses and David, it is clear that it was God who supported and sustained them while operating in their offices. He (God) is still helping all His servants till today. He can help you too.

What Are Your Thoughts?

Apart from Job, did the aforementioned individuals experienced any challenges? Or was it a joy-ride for them throughout? Some further thoughts—what are we supposed to remember when Job's name is mentioned? Why should a non-Israelite (Job) be accorded honour, recognition and great respect by God? Should we expect someone like Job whose profile was outstanding to be excluded from suffering, loss, bereavement, pain and challenges of life? Only God can decide on that one.

Conference Held In Job's Absence

I am sure we remember Job's story very well, but many might find it unbelievable that God acted behind the scene during a brief conference in heaven when He permitted Satan to attack Job the way it happened, read (Job 1:8-12),

> Then the LORD said to Satan, "Have you considered My servant Job, that there is none like him on the earth, a blameless and upright man, one who fears God and shuns evil?" 9 So Satan answered the LORD and said, "Does Job fear God for nothing? 10 Have You not made a hedge around him, around his household, and around all that he has on every side? You have blessed the work of his hands, and his possessions have increased in the land. 11 But now, stretch out Your hand and touch all that he has, and he will surely curse You to Your face!" 12 And the LORD said to Satan,

"Behold, all that he has is in your power; only do not lay a hand on his person." So Satan went out from the presence of the LORD. Job 1:8-12

From the above biblical account, it was a short meeting but not like the type normally hosted in the secular workplace or environment. In the establishment of this world, the type of meeting and the calibre of people who would attend such meetings would matter a lot, be it a corporate, private institution, or government meetings and so on. The nature of the meeting would determine how much preparations required, that is, security arrangements, accommodation, hospitality and entertainments, dignitaries expected to attend, transport and logistics and a lot more.

But amazingly, this God's conference with Satan was organised and held in Job's absence. God presided over the meeting and everything looked good enough for the objectives to be adopted and approved for immediate action. Suddenly, within twenty four hours apart from Job and his wife, Job had nothing significant left in his life, as we read in (Job 1:13-19).

Now there was a day when his sons and daughters were eating and drinking wine in their oldest brother's house; 14 and a messenger came to Job and said, "The oxen were plowing and the donkeys feeding beside them, 15 when the Sabeans raided them and took them away—indeed they have killed the servants with the edge of the sword; and I alone have escaped to tell you!" 16 While he was still speaking, another also came and said, "The fire of God fell from heaven and burned up the sheep and the servants, and consumed them; and I alone have escaped to tell you!"

17 While he *was* still speaking, another also came and said, "The Chaldeans formed three bands, raided the camels and took them away, yes, and killed the servants with the edge of the sword; and I alone have escaped to tell you!" 18 While he *was* still speaking, another also came and said, "Your sons and daughters were eating and drinking wine in their oldest brother's house, 19 and suddenly a great wind came from across the wilderness and struck the four corners of the house, and it fell on the young people, and they are dead; and I alone have escaped to tell you!" Job 1:13-19

Shortly, Satan came back again like Oliver Twist, he asked for 'more' and after another short conference with God, Satan attacked Job's health, (Job 2:3-8).

Then the LORD said to Satan, "Have you considered My servant Job, that there is none like him on the earth, a blameless and upright man, one who fears God and shuns evil? And still he holds fast to his integrity, although you incited Me against him, to destroy him without cause." 4 So Satan answered the LORD and said, "Skin for skin! Yes, all that a man has he will give for his life. 5 But stretch out Your hand now, and touch his bone and his flesh, and he will surely curse You to Your face!" 6 And the LORD said to Satan, "Behold, he is in your hand, but spare his life." 7 So Satan went out from the presence of the LORD, and struck Job with painful boils from the sole of his foot to the crown of his head. 8 And he took for himself a potsherd with which to scrape himself while he sat in the midst of the ashes. 9 Then his wife said to him, "Do you still hold fast to your integrity? Curse God and die!" 10 But he said to her, "You speak as one of the foolish women speaks. Shall we indeed accept good from God, and shall we not accept adversity?" In all this Job did not sin with his lips. Job 2:3-8

That reminds me, exactly as there was a 'Judas' among the twelve disciples of Jesus Christ, so Satan is always present amongst God's children, or have a representative amongst God's children even when they gather in God's presence, something similar to (Job 1:6; 2:1-2).

Now there was a day when the sons of God came to present themselves before the LORD, and Satan also came among ... Job 1:6

Again there was a day when the sons of God came to present themselves before the LORD, and Satan came also among them to present himself before the LORD. 2 And the LORD said to Satan, "From where do you come?" Satan answered the LORD and said, "From going to and fro on the earth, and from walking back and forth on it." Job 2:1-2

God is not a wicked Father, nor takes delight in seeing His children go through suffering and pain. We should understand that God's sovereignty, restorative power, and faithfulness were some of the purposes which made Him to act behind the scene in the above cited texts which involved Job. Importantly, God knew that Job would never allow prosperity to replace God in his life. The devil got it all wrong because Job was not going to be a victim like the two characters in (Genesis 3:1-7), where Eve was easily persuaded and eventually Adam too. They both fell into temptation in the Garden of Eden.

Now the serpent was more cunning than any beast of the field which the LORD God had made. And he said to the woman, "Has God indeed said, 'You shall not eat of every tree of the garden'?" 2 And the woman said to the serpent, "We may eat the fruit of the trees of the garden; 3 but of the fruit of the tree which is in the midst of the garden, God has said, 'You shall not eat it, nor shall you touch it, lest you die.'" 4 Then the serpent said to the woman, "You will not surely die. 5 For God knows that in the day you eat of it your eyes will be opened, and you will be like God, knowing good and evil." 6 So when the woman saw that the tree was good for food, that it was pleasant to the eyes, and a tree desirable to make one wise, she took of its fruit and ate. She also gave to her husband with her, and he ate. 7 Then the eyes of both of them were opened, and they knew that they were naked; and they sewed fig leaves together and made themselves coverings. Genesis 3:1-7

Sadly, today many people worship their 'prosperity' and have allowed it to take the place of God in their lives, that is idolatrous. Also, sometimes God acts behind the scene to show that He is compassionate and merciful, (James 5:11), and will always find a way to rescue His children. Notice that as soon as God's purposes were accomplished, Job's prosperity was restored, (Job 42:10-17),

And the LORD restored Job's losses when he prayed for his friends. Indeed the LORD gave Job twice as much as he had before. 11 Then all his brothers, all his sisters, and all those who had been his acquaintances before, came to him and ate food with him in his house; and they consoled him and comforted him for all the adversity that the LORD had brought upon him. Each one gave him a piece of silver and each a ring of gold. 12 Now the LORD blessed the latter days of Job more than his beginning; for he had fourteen thousand sheep, six thousand camels, one thousand yoke of oxen, and one thousand female donkeys. 13 He also had seven sons and three daughters. 14 And he called the name of the first Jemimah, the name of the second Keziah, and the name of the third Keren-Happuch. 15 In all the land were found no women so beautiful as the daughters of Job; and their father gave them an inheritance among their brothers. 16 After this Job lived one hundred and forty years, and saw his children and grandchildren for four generations. 17 So Job died, old and full of days. Job 42:10-17

Jonah or Job? God's Ultimate Aim Is Fundamental

Whatever the case might be, it should be understood that none of God's servants is prevented from experiencing the challenges that life brings to any mortal person. Succinctly, man or woman, Jonah or Job, we should remember that God's ultimate aim is fundamental, and instead of trying to question Him, it is better to walk in obedience and not allow people to make us sin against God. Learning from Job's experience, we read that his wife in (Job 2:9), and his trusted friends nearly made him to sin against God, as recorded in (Job 42:7-9).

Then his wife said to him, "Do you still hold fast to your integrity? Curse God and die!" Job 2:9

And so it was, after the LORD had spoken these words to Job, that the LORD said to Eliphaz the Temanite,

"My wrath is aroused against you and your two friends, for you have not spoken of Me what is right, as My servant Job has. 8 Now therefore, take for yourselves seven bulls and seven rams, go to My servant Job, and offer up for yourselves a burnt offering; and My servant Job shall pray for you. For I will accept him, lest I deal with you according to your folly; because you have not spoken of Me what is right, as My servant Job has." 9 So Eliphaz the Temanite and Bildad the Shuhite and Zophar the Naamathite went and did as the LORD commanded them; for the LORD had accepted Job. Job 42:7-9

Allow God's Faithfulness To Be Seen

When God's servants or Christian believers go through life's issues, the objective or outcome should be to allow God's faithfulness to be seen in the way they (believers/the servants of God) handle the crisis—this is what brings out God's glory. Don't look for people to pity you. Of course, servants of God, or children of God must readily and willingly depend on God genuinely, without pretence, and rely on this great God with the highest attention and sensitivity, and completely trust in Him who is forever faithful.

Be it known that, every crisis has its own uniqueness, and life span or an expiry date. Therefore, different approaches would be required to handle any situation that occurs, whether it is loss of life, business failure, mental health, divorce or marital problems, to mention a few.

Demonstrate Faith And Trust In God

When believers face difficulties, it is pertinent for them to express and demonstrate faith and trust in God throughout the period the situation lasts for. Typically, Job who lost everything in one day had to trust God even when he suffered ill-health during the crisis. One of the lessons we can learn from his quandary is that, he is a good example of someone who demonstrated faith, trust, patience and confidence in God. Note that, the devil threw everything at him (Job), yet He trusted God.

In contrast, Jonah did not put his faith, trust and confidence in God when he began his journey. Instead, he paid for his transport fare to Tarshish and was unwilling to go to Nineveh where God originally sent him. Surprisingly, in spite of Jonah's disobedience or rebellion, God showed him mercy. Should Christian believers of today emulate Jonah's example or Job? I won't advise anyone to emulate Jonah's disobedient behaviour, because we cannot tell if they would obtain his type of mercy should they go against what God required of them. In a few words, always remember that, Job can be described as a symbol of trust, faith and confidence, one who held strongly to God during his adversity from start to finish. Christian believers would do well with this type of character traits.

Why Should Bad Things Happen To Good People?

At first, the above question can be difficult to answer, but it is not really difficult if we bring God's perspective into it. Job whose name means, to return to God or repent in Arabic, or someone who was 'greatly tried' in Hebrew,[19] was a wealthy man with righteous character who lived and faced overwhelming challenges through no fault of his. To differentiate between Job and Jonah, the latter caused some

---

19 Jamieson, Fausset, & Brown, Commentary on the Whole Bible, Grand Rapids, Michigan: Zondervan Publishing House, 1961, p. 363

temporary, but disastrous problem on himself and his fellow travellers, whereas, Job had no answers to the tragedies that befell him, and he was meant to get on with his life—just like that?

Why should bad things happen to good people? I would say this is a strange situation, but that was how, firstly, it was supposed to be for him to demonstrate that God can be trusted. Secondly, that he (Job) loved God and could use his life to honour God even when he didn't understand what was happening. Thirdly, all Christian believers should note that Job was a non-Israelite who decided to serve Yahweh, being the case, his dilemma which was a terrible incident, can be considered as one of the templates to be borne in mind if we really profess that we love God with all our heart, soul and strength as declared in (Deuteronomy 6:4).

> "Hear, O Israel: The LORD our God, the LORD is one! 5 You shall love the LORD your God with all your heart, with all your soul, and with all your strength. Deuteronomy 6:4

Fourthly, like Job, we should not serve God because of prosperity but true love, and when our faith is tested, we should stand firm and be unshaken in God.

Job Was A Worshipper

We learn about God's faithfulness through this man called Job. He gallantly endured physical drain on his strength, pain, mental fatigue, and wrong accusations through his friends. Instead of discouragement, losing faith and trust in God, we remember him saying on an occasion that, 'I know my Redeemer lives' see (Job 19:25), a testimony that, for him, all was not lost. Also, while terrible losses were all over his life, he turned to God through worship and never sinned against God as recorded in (Job 1:20-22).

> Then Job arose, tore his robe, and shaved his head; and he fell to the ground and worshiped. 21 And he said: "Naked I came from my mother's womb, And naked shall I return there. The LORD gave, and the LORD has taken away; Blessed be the name of the LORD." 22 In all this Job did not sin nor charge God with wrong. Job 1:20-22

God will never owe any person, I know it, because after God's purpose was established, Job was restored twice the original blessings he had, you can refer to (Job 42:12-13), for confirmation. May all my readers be compensated by God having allowed His purpose to come to pass.

> 12 Now the LORD blessed the latter days of Job more than his beginning; for he had fourteen thousand sheep, six thousand camels, one thousand yoke of oxen, and one thousand female donkeys. 13 He also had seven sons and three daughters. Job 42:12-13

It is with great joy and a big relief to see that Job's trouble ended positively. His patience and doggedness cannot be rubbished. If granted, would Jonah allow his life to be exemplary like Job? Would he be happy to see the Ninevites repent? Unfortunately, Jonah had preferred God's judgment to fall on the Israeli aggressor and tormentor without leniency. However. let's find out in the next chapter if Jonah would reason with God and allow his attitude to win the souls of the Ninevites through God's mercy and love.

CHAPTER ELEVEN
RE-DIRECTING NINEVEH TOWARDS GOD'S MERCY AND LOVE

Sitting At The Other End Of The Bench

Jonah was a type of person who wished to see God's burning anger descend and consume the entire inhabitants of Nineveh. At least, that was the impression he gave us, since the time he was sent to warn the Ninevites about the impending doom which awaited them. One of the questions that comes to mind is, has this evangelist received mercy before? If so, why not wish that other people receive God's mercy? For the sake of argument, if Jonah never received mercy before and God decided to show mercy to any community, what has that got to do with him (Jonah)?

Truth be told, there are many people in the world today who are like that. From my pastoral experience I can say that many people were helped and supported during crisis and challenging times, but they never replicated the kind gesture received in the lives of their fellows, what a world! In regards to Jonah, definitely, God had an idea about what to do to re-orientate the former, so that he could be empathetic and merciful towards people as time went by.

However, it was not an easy and straightforward session between him and God. Yahweh had to take Jonah through some tutorial lessons. What amazes me is that, Jonah appeared unconvinced and determined that the destruction of the Assyrians should happen, whereas, God was ready to show mercy, serve them forgiveness and spare their lives. What this meant was that, God was at one end of the bench and Jonah at the other end. Simply, Jonah kept his distance from God. Of course, we know who the winner would be, let us read (Jonah 4:5-11),

> So Jonah went out of the city and sat on the east side of the city. There he made himself a shelter and sat under it in the shade, till he might see what would become of the city. 6 And the LORD God prepared a plant and made it come up over Jonah, that it might be shade for his head to deliver him from his misery. So Jonah was very grateful for the plant. 7 But as morning dawned the next day God prepared a worm, and it so damaged the plant that it withered. 8 And it happened, when the sun arose, that God prepared a vehement east wind; and the sun beat on Jonah's head, so that he grew faint. Then he wished death for himself, and said, "It is better for me to die than to live." 9 Then God said to Jonah, "Is it right for you to be angry about the plant?" And he said, "It is right for me to be angry, even to death!" 10 But the LORD said, "You have had pity on the plant for which you have not labored, nor made it grow, which came up in a night and perished in a night. 11 And should I not pity Nineveh, that great city, in which are more than one hundred and twenty thousand persons who cannot discern between their right hand and their left—and much livestock?" Jonah 4:5-11

Seven Wisdom Snippets To Attract Mercy

1. Undoubtedly Jonah was a servant of God but was insensitive, learn to be sensitive and aspire to make your mark positively, no matter who you are.

137

2. Jonah disobeyed God's instruction and he was over critical of others, be reasonable if you really want to attract God's mercy.

3. Jonah was spared God's instant judgment because of His (God) mercy, but he was not ready to reciprocate this to the Assyrians. Be merciful to other humans so that you can attract God's mercy.

4. The prophet was given an opportunity to learn about how God allows us to be 'humans', be patient with people if you want to attract God's mercy into your life.

5. God gave Jonah the opportunity to see things His (God's) way rationally, and not sentimentally as Jonah wished—be ready to learn and you will see God's mercy shown to you.

6. God shows His reluctance in executing judgment on sinners (the Assyrians in this case), but Jonah wanted it the other way. Don't be too wise in your own eyes, because such behaviour doesn't allow God's mercy to flow into human life.

7. Jonah behaved as if the Ninevites were his personal property, he was wrong. He misunderstood his success, became angry, was frustrated and wished he was dead. However, we all should remember that, true ownership of every good thing comes from God and belongs to Him. Being egoistic will close the doors of mercy against people, avoid this type of behaviour and mercy will flow into your life freely.

One wonders why Jonah should be angry, frustrated and wished he was dead when the original intention of God was to see the Assyrians repented and be saved. The statement from the beginning was very clear, and God saw that the Assyrians repented and He spared them, (Jonah 1:1-3; 3:1-2; 3:10). Let us read,

Now the word of the LORD came to Jonah the son of Amittai, saying, 2 "Arise, go to Nineveh, that great city, and cry out against it; for their wickedness has come up before Me." 3 But Jonah arose to flee to Tarshish from the presence of the LORD. He went down to Joppa, and found a ship going to Tarshish; so he paid the fare, and went down into it, to go with them to Tarshish from the presence of the LORD. Jonah 1:1-3

Now the word of the LORD came to Jonah the second time, saying, 2 "Arise, go to Nineveh, that great city, and preach to it the message that I tell you." Jonah 3:1-2

10 Then God saw their works, that they turned from their evil way; and God relented from the disaster that He had said He would bring upon them, and He did not do it. Jonah 3:10

What supposed to be a success story was either misunderstood, or mis-interpreted by Jonah who wanted the full force of God's judgment to fall on the foreign heathen nation. But God deals with us (humans) differently. The success in this regard was that, repentance was preached by the evangelist (Jonah) who was sent by God with warnings about an imminent destruction to the Ninevites, and they repented. And because they repented, God rescinded the decision, which was better and they received salvation. Unfortunately, Jonah was unhappy and melancholic. It seems Jonah had forgotten that the most important reason behind his mission was to re-direct the Ninevites towards God's mercy and love. To be honest, any of us could get it wrong, or might have gotten it wrong somewhere before now. What shouldn't be allowed is that, after reading this book, no one is permitted to ignore, or try to prevent people from receiving the mercy and love of God.

Imagine God asking Jonah, "What do you want me to do to the Ninevites?" Perhaps, Jonah would have loved for God to destroy them by all means, so that the Ninevites would not call him (Jonah) a liar.

Further, that by God going ahead to destroying the Ninevites, people who hear about the destruction or God's judgment meted out on the Ninevites, would respect him (Jonah), honour him, and his reputation (as 'great evangelist'), would not be at stake.

From the preceding paragraph, you can see that, Jonah's ego mattered most to him and there are many 'Evangelist Jonahs' around our lives today who are mainly concerned about their self-importance. This must stop. Should God's hands be bent or twisted for one's selfish desire? Never! But who can succeed in doing that? Nobody. Who should be in charge, God or man? My response is, God.

College Of Realignment

Sad to say, but presently I have observed that, there is no much difference when people come together. That is, from the pulpit to the pew, there is arrogance, unhealthy rivalry for who should be in-charge, fire the shots, or dictate the tune and so on. My supposition, there is urgent need for all believers in Christ to realign towards God's mercy and love, that we all be humble and allow God to teach us to show mercy, and begin to love the unloved in our society, and community. We all should be ready to attend a 'College of

Realignment' relevant to our circumstance like God did to Jonah, refer to (Jonah 4:4-11). Let us read,

> 4 Then the LORD said, "Is it right for you to be angry?" 5 So Jonah went out of the city and sat on the east side of the city. There he made himself a shelter and sat under it in the shade, till he might see what would become of the city. 6 And the LORD God prepared a plant and made it come up over Jonah, that it might be shade for his head to deliver him from his misery. So Jonah was very grateful for the plant. 7 But as morning dawned the next day God prepared a worm, and it so damaged the plant that it withered. 8 And it happened, when the sun arose, that God prepared a vehement east wind; and the sun beat on Jonah's head, so that he grew faint. Then he wished death for himself, and said, "It is better for me to die than to live." 9 Then God said to Jonah, "Is it right for you to be angry about the plant?" And he said, "It is right for me to be angry, even to death!" 10 But the LORD said, "You have had pity on the plant for which you have not labored, nor made it grow, which came up in a night and perished in a night. 11 And should I not pity Nineveh, that great city, in which are more than one hundred and twenty thousand persons who cannot discern between their right hand and their left—and much livestock?" Jonah 4:4-11

Seven Tough And Difficult Questions For Every Believer

After reading the above scripture (Jonah 4:4-11), we should be ready to ask and answer seven tough and difficult questions about ourselves, personal motives, and ministry, if we truly want to be God's ambassadors for this century and beyond.

1. Jonah had wanted everything to be done as he deemed fit. However, given a choice, should we continue to see things God's way, or our way? Think about at least, one time in your life when you did things your own way. I am guilty in this regard and I repent, let God forgive me. What about you?
2. As a believer, do you really treat people as God would have treated them, or you treat them as you think they deserve to be treated? Do you find it difficult to forgive people easily, or you find it difficult to overlook things? Remember how Jonah attended believers orientation college and repent quickly.
3. Would anyone like to agree that they share some resemblance with Jonah in their attitude? In what ways are you prepared to rectify this? Are you the type that accepts when you are wrong? See (Luke 15:18),

    18 I will arise and go to my father, and will say to him, "Father, I have sinned against heaven and before you. Luke 15:18

4. Would you like God to treat you the same way you treat others? Hear what (Luke 6:37) says,

    37 "Judge not, and you shall not be judged. Condemn not, and you shall not be condemned. Forgive, and you will be forgiven. Luke 6:37

Jonah didn't realise that by shunning God's assignment when he headed towards Tarshish he was acting in a complete disobedience. Have you disobeyed God in the past? What is your opinion for doing that?

5. Should God who forgave Jonah not be permitted to forgive others—what do you think? Should God who forgave you not be allowed to forgive others? It's tough, isn't it? Forgive, pray and release the individual who offended you. Let them go.

6. That God had shown Jonah mercy, should that same God not be allowed to show mercy to other people and nations if need be? Has God done something in the past to make you feel angry, uncomfortable, unhappy, and jealous? You need to prayerfully find out what was in His mind. Remember (Romans 8:28),

> 28 And we know that all things work together for good to those who love God, to those who are the called according to His purpose. Romans 8:28

7. Why should Jonah fail to understand that God who spared his life should be allowed to spare others? To yourself, why should you fail to understand that God who spared your life should be allowed to spare others? Think before you answer. You had wished that some people were dead, but they are still alive, especially the wicked ones. God might be directing them towards His mercy and love, that is why you need to be patient and let God handle it.

Let God Handle It

Typically, there is a parable in the New Testament titled, The Parable of the Unforgiving Servant. In that story, there was a servant who was forgiven so much, but he refused to forgive the other person who owed him a little money, (Matthew 18:28-34). Of course, God handled the matter and the consequence of the latter's action was great. Let us read,

28 "But that servant went out and found one of his fellow servants who owed him a hundred denarii; and he laid hands on him and took him by the throat, saying, 'Pay me what you owe!' 29 So his fellow servant fell down at his feet and begged him, saying, 'Have patience with me, and I will pay you all.' 30 And he would not, but went and threw him into prison till he should pay the debt. 31 So when his fellow servants saw what had been done, they were very grieved, and came and told their master all that had been done. 32 Then his master, after he had called him, said to him, 'You wicked servant! I forgave you all that debt because you begged me. 33 Should you not also have had compassion on your fellow servant, just as I had pity on you?' 34 And his master was angry, and delivered him to the torturers until he should pay all that was due to him. Matthew 18:28-34

It is possible to have behaved at some point in our lives like the unforgiving servant in the above scripture, or like Jonah. However, because of God's love and His compassion that fails not, we can turn to Him for a better orientation. Candidly, God abounds in mercy and He is always forgiving, He suspended the rule when it was Jonah's turn to face the consequences of his disobedience, as it was recorded, "The soul who sins shall die. The son shall not bear the guilt of the father, nor the father bear the guilt of the son, (Ezekiel 18:20a). Yet, God preserved Jonah. Do you think Jonah would have stood any chance?

In regards to the original context in which the foregoing statement was made, (Ezekiel 18:20), God was speaking to Ezekiel about the extent of godlessness, lawlessness and non-compliance to God's rules which was prevalent among God's people—the Israelites. They had adopted their own philosophical and personal ethical conducts which they deemed better than what God had given them, forgetting about personal responsibility and accountability to Yahweh who was their God whom they supposed to be accountable to.

Was Jonah any different? And again, did Jonah stand any chance at all? Are we any better as ministers, professionals, teachers, students, CEOs, parents, and so on? Arguably, could one say that Jonah was strong enough to admit his mistakes? There is no indication in his book to suggest that. Rather, he expressed his anger and frustration to God, (Jonah 4:9-11). Let us read,

> 9 Then God said to Jonah, "Is it right for you to be angry about the plant?" And he said, "It is right for me to be angry, even to death!" 10 But the LORD said, "You have had pity on the plant for which you have not labored, nor made it grow, which came up in a night and perished in a night. 11 And should I not pity Nineveh, that great city, in which are more than one hundred and twenty thousand persons who cannot discern between their right hand and their left—and much livestock?" Jonah 4:4-11

Perhaps, a different thoughts should have been given if there were underlying factors that led to Jonah's behaviour. However, we are aware about the historical and political issues which existed between the two nations. In retrospect, the Assyrians were oppressive rulers and tormented the Israelites as a nation during that time. The underlying reasons made it difficult for Jonah to be ready to take responsibility for his behaviour. Secondly, he never showed a character of someone who could overcome adversity that follows them through mercy and love. We have some people like that in our families, churches, offices, and at other places in our lives. What do we do?

Such individuals need our patience, and we need to dialogue with them as God demonstrated when He engaged Jonah in the above cited scripture, (Jonah 4:4-11). Also, we need to pray for them, and as God never gave up on Jonah, so we must not give up on those who behave like 'Jonah' around us. They have to be re-orientated through love and let mercy be shown to them so that they can be on their feet again. Much as I believe in healing miracles and the power of God to heal, but where mental health issues are involved, people should respect the law of the land and they should be encouraged to seek professional/medical advice as required.

Let Us Imagine

The biblical account stated that Jonah boarded the ship going the opposite direction, supposed that was an indication about his mental, emotional and psychological state at the time? Would you expect any good decision or judgment from an individual like that? Someone whose life was facing the opposite direction? Further, after entering the ship, it was recorded that Jonah went to the lower deck and slept in a dark room. Could that possibly be indicative of someone whose life was disintegrating, falling apart, things were going low and becoming gloomy, or depressed? If he was a friend, family or a church member, would you not do something about it? I trust you would have done something. Pray like this,

My Father, my Father, don't let my life disintegrate (personally, spiritually, and mentally) in the name of Jesus Christ

Lord God Almighty, don't let me face the wrong direction in all my endeavours throughout my life, in the name of Jesus Christ

Almighty Father, don't let me take any wrong decision at this stage of my life, in the name of Jesus Christ

My Father and my God, make me a good and obedient person from this moment in the name of Jesus Christ of Nazareth.

Go ahead after the prayers and give thanks and praises for everything He has done, what He is doing, and the ones you trust Him to do in your life. We cannot exhaust the list of our requests or desires before God so long as we live. Is there anything left to say or do? There is room and opportunity to say to our Maker, at least, "Just One thing, Lord!" Be assured, He will not ignore you—put your trust in Him.

CHAPTER TWELVE
JUST ONE THING, LORD!

The Prominent One

There's always one prominent thing that God uses to announce, promote and launch His children to stardom. The "one thing" could be your skill, talent, anointing, zeal for the things of God, being good in a particular subject at school, the gift of singing, evangelism, and preaching, cooking a particular meal, knowing how to talk to young people and they listen to you, repairing gadgets and so on. God does that intentionally and decisively as we have seen in the ministry of some selected individuals below. Namely, Moses, Joseph, David, Elijah, Daniel, Shadrach, Meshach, and AbedNego to mention but a few. Would Jonah allow God to use the "one thing" in his life for the Ninevites? For Jonah, the 'one thing' was for him to go and evangelise the Ninevites. A short account on the aforementioned names as referenced below testifies to how awesome God is.

Moses — He confronted Pharaoh (Exodus 12:30-32) when God changed his status prior. The power of Egypt was never a match to this one-time murderer and a runaway individual. God used this past fugitive to lead the Israelites from the Egyptian bondage after over four hundred years. Despite his unattractive C.V, God knew that Moses would be committed to His deliverance project.

> So Pharaoh rose in the night, he, all his servants, and all the Egyptians; and there was a great cry in Egypt,

for there was not a house where there was not one dead. 31 Then he called for Moses and Aaron by night, and said, "Rise, go out from among my people, both you and the children of Israel. And go, serve the LORD as you have said. 32 Also take your flocks and your herds, as you have said, and be gone; and bless me also." Exodus 12:30-32

Joseph — He interpreted Pharaoh's dream according to (Genesis 41:38-41), although he was a slave in the past, and a prisoner through no crime committed. But God used the gift of the interpretation of dreams to announce him and suddenly he became a powerful personality whose authority could not be questioned in the land of Egypt.

And Pharaoh said to his servants, "Can we find such a one as this, a man in whom is the Spirit of God?" 39 Then Pharaoh said to Joseph, "Inasmuch as God has shown you all this, there is no one as discerning and wise as you. 40 You shall be over my house, and all my people shall be ruled according to your word; only in regard to the throne will I be greater than you." 41 And Pharaoh said to Joseph, "See, I have set you over all the land of Egypt." Genesis 41:38-41

David — He killed Goliath of Gath through the power of God around age twenty which was an extraordinary achievement, (1 Samuel 17:49-51). He was a peasant farmer and a shepherd, and an anointed singer who could minister in songs to stabilise King Saul's mental illness. Furthermore, from a simple and ordinary young man, God empowered him and he became the king of Israel. Moreover, the Messiah came through his lineage (Matthew 1:6, 16), and the rest is history. This is what God can do by using 'one thing' in the lives of His children.

Then David put his hand in his bag and took out a stone; and he slung it and struck the Philistine in his forehead, so that the stone sank into his forehead, and he fell on his face to the earth. 50 So David prevailed over the Philistine with a sling and a stone, and struck the Philistine and killed him. But there was no sword in the hand of David. 51 Therefore David ran and stood over the Philistine, took his sword and drew it out of its sheath and killed him, and cut off his head with it. And when the Philistines saw that their champion was dead, they fled. 1 Samuel 17:49-51

Elijah — When Israel became idolatrous, Elijah declared a compulsory drought and called for fire to settle the case between him and the prophets of Baal on Mount Carmel. Definitely, a super phenomenal encounter to watch based on the biblical account provided, (1 Kings 18:36-39). Note that, King Ahab was part of the audience and God used the occasion to announce Elijah, his servant. Apart from that, He (God) honoured Himself openly and publicly when idolatry was eradicated suddenly because of the way He manifested Himself through the descended fire. God can use any method to promote His children before anybody. Are you ready? Ask God to activate that 'one thing' that will shoot you to fame today.

And it came to pass, at the time of the offering of the evening sacrifice, that Elijah the prophet came near and said, "LORD God of Abraham, Isaac, and Israel, let it be known this day that You are God in Israel and I am Your servant, and that I have done all these things at Your word. 37 Hear me, O LORD, hear me, that this people may know that You are the LORD God, and that You have turned their hearts back to You again." 38 Then the fire of the LORD fell and consumed the burnt sacrifice, and the wood and the stones and the dust, and it licked up the water that was in the trench. 39 Now when all the people saw it, they fell on their faces; and they said, "The LORD, He is God! The LORD, He is God!" 1 Kings 18:36-39

Daniel, Shadrach, Meshach, and AbedNego — These four young men were deported to Babylon. They never compromised their faith in God, despite the absence of their parents, or any senior adult from their background who could mentor or nurture them. They allowed God to use the wisdom and knowledge He blessed them with, to take them to the pinnacle of their political and diplomatic career, (Daniel 1:17-20; 2:46-49a). Their faith in God and their firm believe in Him was unmatchable.

Have you discovered your 'one thing' yet? Importantly, the name of God became known and revered throughout the time they (the four young men) served in the Babylonian and Persian government. You can use your gift, skill or your God-given "one thing," to create impact on earth for God and the benefit of humanity.

As for these four young men, God gave them knowledge and skill in all literature and wisdom; and Daniel had understanding in all visions and dreams. 18 Now at the end of the days, when the king had said that they should be brought in, the chief of the eunuchs brought them in before Nebuchadnezzar. 19 Then the king interviewed them, and among them all none was found like Daniel, Hananiah, Mishael, and Azariah; therefore, they served before the king. 20 And in all matters of wisdom and understanding about which the king examined them, he found them ten times better than all the magicians and astrologers who were in all his realm. Daniel 1:17-20

Then King Nebuchadnezzar fell on his face, prostrate before Daniel, and commanded that they should present an offering and incense to him. 47 The king answered Daniel, and said, "Truly your God is the God of gods, the Lord of kings, and a revealer of secrets, since you could reveal this secret." 48 Then the king promoted Daniel and gave him many great gifts; and he made him ruler over the whole province of Babylon, and chief administrator over all the wise men of Babylon. 49 Also Daniel petitioned the king, and he set Shadrach, Meshach, and Abed-Nego over the affairs of the province of Babylon. Daniel 2:46-49a

Back To Jonah's Story

This same God used 'one thing' or an event, to announce Jonah who was sent to Nineveh. No matter how terrible Jonah behaved, his name has become synonymous with Nineveh. It is impossible to change, or take away this identity from him. I pray that God would give you your "one thing" that would announce you favourably, globally and permanently from today in the name of Jesus Christ.

Why should God go to this extent? The reason behind that "one thing" that spurred God into action, and made Him to not forsake His people, but instead, caused interventions for all the characters we know in the Bible is mercy, (Nehemiah 9:19). Let us read,

Yet in Your manifold mercies You did not forsake them in the wilderness. The pillar of the cloud did not depart from them by day, To lead them on the road; Nor the pillar of fire by night, To show them light, And the way they should go. Nehemiah 9:19

May the mercies of God be your portion from today.

Prayer Points

The Shepherd of Israel! give me that "one thing" that won't let my life to be the same again from now, in the name of Jesus Christ

— That "one thing" that will grant me instant miracles locate me now
— That "one thing" that will guarantee my success, my Father, grant me today
— God of Abraham, give me that "one thing" that will turn around my life and my family positively
— God of all possibilities, grant me that "one thing" that will turn around my endeavours successfully
— That "one thing" Jehovah, that will turn around my marriage greatly, be given to me forever
— That "one thing" that will turn around my children's life positively, be given to them
— That "one thing" that will turn around my family's life favourably, be given to us
— That "one thing" that will turn around my ministry successfully, be given to me, Lord
— That "one thing" that will turn around my business and cause it to prosper, be given to me
— My Father, my Father, give me that "one thing" that will turn around my life permanently for good, in the name of Jesus Christ

The Stone of Israel! make me a household name that will glorify your name from today in the name of Jesus Christ

God of Israel! make me a household name for your glory from today, in the name of Jesus Christ

The Great Covenant-keeper! let my name be heard where it matters most, from today and for your glory in the name of Jesus Christ

God of Abraham! let my contact details be known where it matters most, from today for your glory and for my good, in the name of Jesus Christ

God of Isaac! let the contact details of my ministry be known and rewarded, where it matters most in the name of Jesus Christ

God of Jacob! let the contact details of my business be presented and rewarded, where it matters most in the name of Jesus Christ

God, who related on a personal level with Jonah despite his initial disobedience:

— Relate on a personal level to me in regards to my health and make me whole, in the name of Jesus Christ
— Relate on a personal level to me in regards to my marriage in the name of Jesus Christ
— Relate on a personal level to me in regards to my vocation/career/education in the name of Jesus Christ
— Relate on a personal level to me in regards to my finances, and make me debt-free in the name of Jesus Christ

God who related on a personal level to Jonah, connect me to my destiny helpers, and let my life get better from this moment, in the name of Jesus Christ

— Let the life of my spouse get better
— Let the life of my children get better
— Let the life of my entire family get better in the name of Jesus Christ

Almighty Father! you picked up Jonah and showed him mercy, be merciful to me from now in the name of Jesus Christ. My Father, my Father, You said, "I will be gracious to whom I will be gracious, and I will have compassion on whom I will have compassion." (Exodus 33:19b),

Merciful Father, pick me up and qualify me for your abundant mercies in the name of Jesus Christ

— Qualify my family
— Qualify my business
— Qualify my career
— Qualify my ministry
— Qualify me financially
— Qualify me materially and all-round for your glory, in the name of Jesus Christ.

The "Nineveh" assignment announced the destiny of Jonah, Holy Spirit of God, grant me what will announce my destiny gloriously from today, in the name of Jesus Christ

The "Nineveh" assignment announced the destiny of Jonah, Holy Spirit of God, give me what will announce my destiny globally from today in the name of Jesus Christ

The "Nineveh" assignment announced the destiny of Jonah, Holy Spirit of God, do what will announce my endeavours gloriously and globally from today, in the name of Jesus Christ

Jonah fumbled at the beginning of his assignment, but You helped him, Almighty Father, help me to accomplish my mission in life, because of your mercy in the name of Jesus Christ

— Father, help me to accomplish spiritually
— Help me to accomplish vocationally
— Help me to accomplish in ministry
— Help me to accomplish in all my endeavours
— Help me to accomplish in raising my children in God's way in the name of Jesus Christ

Almighty Father, you helped Jonah, help me to finish well, because of your mercy in the name of Jesus Christ

— Help my spouse to finish well
— Help my entire family to finish well
— Help my children to finish well in the name of Jesus Christ

The ordained miracles of God allocated to my destiny, begin to reveal yourselves now, in the name of Jesus Christ

— Reveal yourselves to me in the name of Jesus Christ

The ordained miracles of God apportioned to my life, I am available, locate me now, in the name of Jesus Christ

— I am available, locate me now in the name of Jesus Christ

God Almighty who helped Jonah, don't let me drown in the ocean of the wicked, spiritually and physically in the name of Jesus Christ

— Don't let me drown materially and medically in the ocean of the wicked in the name of Jesus Christ
— Don't let my spouse drown in the ocean of the wicked
— Don't let my children drown in the ocean of the wicked
— Don't let me and my loved ones drown in the ocean of the wicked
— Don't let my business drown in the ocean of the wicked
— Don't let me drown in the ocean of financial debts
— Don't let my business drown in the ocean of sickness and disease
— Don't let my ministry drown in the ocean of the wicked in the name of Jesus Christ

Thank you Lord for answering my prayers, may Your name be forever praised, Hallelujah!

God who re-directed the Ninevites to Himself through His mercy and love, had in the past used one thing or the other, to glorify His name in the lives of some biblical individuals like, Moses, Joseph, David, Elijah, Shadrach, Meshach, and Abednego, to mention this few. He is ready to show you mercy. He knows what to do. We shall learn about how mercy can be available to you too, in the next chapter.

CHAPTER THIRTEEN
MERCY IS AVAILABLE FOR YOU TOO

Mercy

As it was during Jonah's time, mercy is certainly available and God can be merciful to you too. I believe so, because once upon a time, God spoke to Moses that He would show him mercy and He did, (Exodus 33:19). This was not because Moses was perfect, intelligent, strong or superior, but God chose to do so willingly. May God be merciful to you from now.

> And he said, I will make all my goodness pass before thee, and I will proclaim the name of the LORD before thee; and will be gracious to whom I will be gracious, and will shew mercy on whom I will shew mercy.
> Exodus 33:19 AV

What is mercy? Mercy is the instrument that prevents God from dishing out the punishment that humanity deserve for their sins. In the absence of mercy, people should expect the wrath or punishment that our sins deserve from God. In another way, mercy can be defined as, to be kind, and compassionate. It includes forgiveness, love and sympathy. All these are available to us from God.

What to do in response? We should walk in obedience, be passionate like Moses and other patriarchs and matriarchs did, and be devoted to God and the things He has entrusted to us. By that, we can be attracted to Him and foster a better and intimate relationship which can bring us to where we are supposed to be in our relationship with Him (God). Additionally, we have to be genuine in our walk with Him. However, He has the exclusive right to show mercy at any time and to anyone He decides, (Exodus 33:19, cf. Romans 9:14-16),

> What shall we say then? Is there unrighteousness with God? Certainly not! 15 For He says to Moses, "I will have mercy on whomever I will have mercy, and I will have compassion on whomever I will have compassion." 16 So then it is not of him who wills, nor of him who runs, but of God who shows mercy." Romans 9:14-16

Mercy Is Not By Human Efforts

There are many instances in the Bible that demonstrate God's merciful nature, therefore, be assured that the mercy of God is available to you too. As you would find below, there are many scriptures provided to show the diverse ways in which God's mercies can be bestowed on you, but not through your efforts. Do you think God's mercy is far away from you? That His mercy is impossible to reach you where you are? That it's too late to redeem your condition? It isn't too late, with God all things are possible.

Here are some more thoughts for you: Do you think you are gone past the age bracket in which mercy can be shown to you? That you are unreachable due to your location, status, gender or race? Or, because of what some people said, mercy is beyond your reach? Your guess or their guess is wrong because no excuse can deter God when He is ready to show mercy to any person. Further, it could be that you or they, are wrong because of the below narration that I am about to share with you. Mercy is available for you and is obtainable once God is ready.

Ten Selected Recipients of Mercy

Some of the biblical recipients of mercy include, the Mad man of Gadara (Luke 8:26-39), the woman at Canaan (Matthew 15:22-28), the parent with an epileptic son (Matthew 17:15), the two blind men (Matthew 20:30-34), blind Bartimaeus (Mark 10:46-52), Elizabeth was shown great mercy (Luke 1:50-58), a robbery victim (Luke 10:30-37), the ten lepers (Luke 17:11-14), feeding the four thousand (Matthew 15:32-38), and the widow at Nain (Luke 7:11-15).

The story regarding the above ten individually selected recipients of God's mercy will encourage you, and challenge your faith to expect mercy from God. It is the message about individuals showcasing God's compassion and this same God, will be merciful to you from now onwards. Let us start with the story of the mad man at Gadara. A mad man? Yes. His dilemma that Jesus turned around for him should encourage your heart for various reasons (Luke 8:26-39).

The mad man called himself—Legion

We do not know how he came about that name or understanding, but Collins Dictionary & Thesaurus defines it as, a unit of three to six thousand men in the ancient Roman army. So, for the mad man to call himself Legion, it shows that he was truly possessed by many demons. Notwithstanding, he was shown mercy on an appointed day and his life changed completely. I pray for mercy for you in the name of Jesus Christ. Let us read his story in (Luke 8:26-39).

Then they sailed to the country of the Gadarenes, which is opposite Galilee. 27 And when He (Jesus) stepped out on the land, there met Him a certain man from the city who had demons for a long time. And he wore no clothes, nor did he live in a house but in the tombs. 28 When he saw Jesus, he cried out, fell down before Him, and with a loud voice said, "What have I to do with You, Jesus, Son of the Most High God? I beg You, do not torment me!" 29 For He had commanded the unclean spirit to come out of the man. For it had often seized him, and he was kept under guard, bound with chains and shackles; and he broke the bonds and was driven by the demon into the wilderness. 30 Jesus asked him, saying, "What is your name?" And he said, "Legion," because many demons had entered him. 31 And they begged Him that He would not command them to go out into the abyss. 32 Now a herd of many swine was feeding there on the mountain. So they begged Him that He would permit them to enter them. And He permitted them. 33 Then the demons went out of the man and entered the swine, and the herd ran violently down the steep place into the lake and drowned. 34 When those who fed them saw what had happened, they fled and told it in the city and in the country. 35 Then they went out to see what had happened, and came to Jesus, and found the man from whom the demons had departed, sitting at the feet of Jesus, clothed and in his right mind. And they were afraid. 36 They also who had seen it told them by what means he who had been demon-possessed was healed.

37 Then the whole multitude of the surrounding region of the Gadarenes asked Him to depart from them, for they were seized with great fear. And He got into the boat and returned. 38 Now the man from whom the demons had departed begged Him that he might be with Him. But Jesus sent him away, saying, 39 "Return to your own house, and tell what great things God has done for you." And he went his way and proclaimed throughout the whole city what great things Jesus had done for him. Luke 8:26-39

I know that people can either be insensitive, or selfish towards one another, but the mad man's story should stimulate your faith and prepare your heart to be ready for your miracles on the platform of mercy. The condition of the demoniac was so terrible that people concluded for example, that:

- It was impossible for him to be healed of his madness
- It was impossible for him to be absorbed back into the society
- He had nothing to offer his generation in terms of gift, skill, talent or relevance
- He would die in that hopelessly, deplorable and helpless condition, and so on.

However, they were wrong because the mad man was on God's VIPs list for the day Jesus went to meet him at the cemetery. Amazingly, he was the only person Jesus healed in the entire neighbourhood on the day. What does that imply? Three things to note:

- That shows that the demoniac was important to God, even when he meant nothing to the people around him.

- For Jesus to have permitted two thousand pigs to perish in the sea for the sake of the mad man, this should be deemed as a signal that there was something special God had put in the life of the demoniac that is beyond the ordinary mind.
- Jesus left the city after healing the mad man, this is a testimony that the demoniac had a place in God's heart, so much that God could not afford to let him remain in that condition beyond that day. Indeed, God was mindful of him as the psalmist says in (Psalm 8:3-4).

When I consider Your heavens, the work of Your fingers, The moon and the stars, which You have ordained, 4 What is man that You are mindful of him, And the son of man that You visit him? Psalm 8:3-4

May your case receive urgent, personal and favourable attention from God from today in the name of Jesus Christ.

360 Degree Turnaround

The man in the above cited scripture had too many problems. He was insane, jobless, homeless, and indeed his future looked bleak and forfeited. He was separated from his family due to his affliction. That could mean somebody taken away from their marriage, business, ministry, and profession, against their will. The best place he was residing at the time, was in a tomb in a cemetery. What is more, it is appropriate to say that, he was like a human living in a remote island. It was a 'rent-free' solitary confinement, or accommodation which no sane person would desire to live.

Further, he was an individual that was living in isolation with so many demons troubling his life. Additionally, it is right to say that the place he saw as his home was uninhabitable to normal human beings. Could such a person be expected to receive help or mercy? Yet, one day the mercy of God found him through what I call, "Appointment with the Custodian of Mercy," and suddenly everything in his life changed for the better. The next time the public saw him, he was no longer naked, not dirty or unkempt, but clothed and was back in his right mind, (Luke 8:35). For short, that was a 360 degree (360°) turnaround. May God turnaround your entire life positively, in the name of Jesus Christ.

> Then they went out to see what had happened, and came to Jesus, and found the man from whom the demons had departed, sitting at the feet of Jesus, clothed and in his right mind. And they were afraid. Luke 8:35

Notice that Jesus travelled to the region without any invitation—that was mercy in action. Also, remember that the man was demon-possessed for many years. Therefore, it is not a bad idea to assume that the man could have died in that condition, yet mercy preserved him until Jesus went there. As if that was not enough, mercy spoke for him and his entire life was reversed favourably. May mercy speak for you where they have written you off. Realise that in the past, the man had no dignity, he had no sense of pain, hence he cut himself anyhow. Beyond any doubt, he was dead to the pain, but Jesus reversed his entire condition. There is hope for you.

Presently, there are people who have suffered for so long that they don't feel the 'pain' any more. Be assured, mercy is available for you too. In a nutshell, once upon a time, the demoniac was naked, isolated, separated from his family, confined to the cemetery, and vulnerable to the extent that the demons were dictating to him what to do to his physical body. He was never in control of his life until Jesus came (uninvited) to set him free. Mercy is available for you too, and may mercy intervene for you and set you free in the name of Jesus Christ.

Seven Moral Lessons From The Demoniac's Meeting

- Every human life is important to God
- Every human suffering or dilemma that has a beginning, has expiry date
- Nobody has a right to tell God how to end the challenge in your life
- Never say 'never' as a result of people's present condition or status, because God can cause a miracle to happen any time
- It was recorded that two thousand pigs were destroyed (Mark 5:13) by the demons that left the demoniac's body. Truthfully, the man was in a deep trouble before Jesus exorcised the demons, but see the end result—Jesus came and set the captive free.
- That saved soul through Jesus is important to God than thousands of swine at any particular time. Note that soon, Jesus, the only begotten Son of God would die on the Cross at Calvary for the souls of all mankind including the swine keepers and the demoniac that He recently healed.
- Arguably, critics would say the swine keepers lost their means of livelihood. Always remember that, the souls of mankind is very important to God than economic benefits, so much that soon after that event, God used Jesus to pay the price for the redemption of humanity by going to the Cross. This is important, it does not matter who were the swine keepers—Gentiles or Jews, but if they were Jews, it means they were operating illegally and dealing in unclean business. And who knows, may be after the incident they would go and deal legally in clean business.

The demoniac was healed as a single person, but the effect was massive, touching the community, his friends, family, believers and unbelievers of the time. Notice this, his miraculous healing was enough to evangelise people to church. The devil lost it when his (the demoniac) life was transformed. May your latter days be better than the beginning. Let's see what we can learn from the second recipient of mercy.

Man or Woman, Cry For Mercy—It's free of charge!

Bartimaeus was a man that won't keep quiet because he knew from experience that keeping quiet would mean missing great opportunities for alms. He had nothing to lose, but a lot to gain hence he cried the more, and he was right— he was healed at last. Man or woman, cry for mercy, it is free of charge. Fancy a woman who did that too? She came from Canaan the same region where Jesus turned water to wine.

The Woman From Canaan, (Matthew 15:22-28)

The people around Jesus' region of birth where the woman from Canaan came from, didn't have faith in Him, for that reason He (Jesus) didn't do many miracles among them, (Mark 6:4-6). Let us read,

> 4 But Jesus said to them, "A prophet is not without honor except in his own country, among his own relatives, and in his own house." 5 Now He could do no mighty work there, except that He laid His hands on a few sick people and healed them. 6 And He marveled because of their unbelief. Then He went about the villages in a circuit, teaching. Mark 6:4-6

But, the woman was an exception, she had faith in Jesus and her demon-possessed daughter was healed. Let us read (Matthew 15:22-28),

22 And behold, a woman of Canaan came from that region and cried out to Him, saying, "Have mercy on me, O Lord, Son of David! My daughter is severely demon-possessed." 23 But He answered her not a word. And His disciples came and urged Him, saying, "Send her away, for she cries out after us." 24 But He answered and said, "I was not sent except to the lost sheep of the house of Israel." 25 Then she came and worshiped Him, saying, "Lord, help me!" 26 But He answered and said, "It is not good to take the children's bread and throw it to the little dogs." 27 And she said, "Yes, Lord, yet even the little dogs eat the crumbs which fall from their masters' table." 28 Then Jesus answered and said to her, "O woman, great is your faith! Let it be to you as you desire." And her daughter was healed from that very hour. Matthew 15:22-28

The woman in question could have come from any part of the world, town, or city. What makes her story interesting is that, she was determined for a turnaround, and was ready to bear the consequences of a social stigma, or stereotype which was historical in nature. Was it a test of her faith? Was it a test of her patience, or ability to look beyond a derogatory remark? Was it the ability to get one's priority right, and be ready to pay the price for what it takes to obtain mercy? Perhaps we would never know.

However, one of the things that sets her apart, is her ability and power to put prejudice aside. She was resilient, humble, and she engaged Jesus constructively and directly. What to do from now? Learn to persevere at the place of prayer, and tarry in the presence of the Holy Spirit like the woman did with Jesus.

Notice that she did not come with self-pity, but showed her hunger, thirst, and desperation for mercy. Suddenly, the conversation between her and the Saviour of the world took a favourable twist for her, as confirmed in (Matthew 15:27-28), what are you waiting for?

> 27 And she said, "Yes, Lord, yet even the little dogs eat the crumbs which fall from their masters' table." 28 Then Jesus answered and said to her, "O woman, great is your faith! Let it be to you as you desire." Matthew 15:27-28

May God hear your plea today in the name of Jesus Christ. As you engage in your prayer for mercy, may you receive mercy that would change your life forever, like the woman from Canaan. Further, one of the moral lessons to bear in mind is that, people should learn to swallow their pride, so that they can receive mercy quickly, and for where it is most needed.

Pray like this: Mercy of God, fall on me, fall on every member of my family, fall on my marriage, fall on my career, fall on my ministry, fall on all my endeavours, in the name of Jesus Christ. Amen! This marks the end of the story of the second recipient, let us turn to the third receiver.

The Agonising Parent, (Matthew 17:15)

I remember the pain and the agony of keeping a vigil beside a sick person at the hospital when a loved one was ill. Such hospital beds especially in the Western world are within a secure location, a warm and hygienic area. However, as narrated in the story, it is a different story when a sick child who suffered from epilepsy fell into the fire and water in the public, and in an open place where no one could guarantee his safety. Hear the wail of the parent, (Matthew 17:15),

15 "Lord, have mercy on my son, for he is an epileptic and suffers severely; for he often falls into the fire and often into the water. Matthew 17:15

As recounted, many times the attack happened without warning signs, and thus exposed the child to terrible dangers, which included, severe burns and a possibility of suffocation in water. Regardless, mercy was available and answered for him one day. Today is your day. Oh, may mercy answer for you in the name of Jesus Christ. Is the tide of life tossing you around, or someone you know? Say this prayer repetitively— Mercy of God, enter my case and grant me unusual miracles in the name of Jesus Christ.

The stories of the first, second, and third recipients ended well, so shall your story be, in the name of Jesus Christ. Next, is the story of the fourth receiver of mercy.

Comrade In Illness, (Matthew 20:30-34)

It appears that the two blind men in (Matthew 20:30-34), knew that the Messiah would be a descendant of David, hence they cried, "Have mercy on us, O Lord, Son of David!" Impliedly, they were saying to Jesus, "please deal with us compassionately." Once they had uttered such remark, they were ready to wait and see what would happen.

Presumably, they had become friends because of the loss of their physical sight. They could understand the daily toll or challenges, and the frustration their condition which was a common denominator between the two of them, had on them. Another common ground was that, both of them were willing to find a solution to their plight. So, when the opportunity came their way, they did not hesitate to act. Their expectation did not fail. May the opportunity that will bless your life come your way as you are reading this book. Thank God, they did not resign to their fate because what they were hoping for, came to pass. Let us read (Matthew 20:30-34),

> 30 And behold, two blind men sitting by the road, when they heard that Jesus was passing by, cried out, saying, "Have mercy on us, O Lord, Son of David!" 31 Then the multitude warned them that they should be quiet; but they cried out all the more, saying, "Have mercy on us, O Lord, Son of David!" 32 So Jesus stood still and called them, and said, "What do you want Me to do for you?" 33 They said to Him, "Lord, that our eyes may be opened." 34 So Jesus had compassion and touched their eyes. And immediately their eyes received sight, and they followed Him. Matthew 20:30-34

What did the blind men do? They called on the name of Jesus, He stood still and He asked them a question, and from there Jesus had compassion on them. Mercy will locate you as you present your prayer requests to God from today. What happened to the two blind men was like an individual granted the opportunity to be hosted by the CEO of an organisation before being employed for work. Fortunately, they were successful and were handed their hypothetical 'letter of employment'. What a joy! May the mercy of God open your eyes to the truth and wisdom of God, things that will bless your life, and answer for you all around, from now in the name of Jesus Christ.

To sum up, the two blind men could be deemed as representing the believing remnant of blinded Israel that would acknowledge Jesus when He returns to reign, (Romans 11:25-26), may we not be left out.[20]

> 25 For I do not desire, brethren, that you should be ignorant of this mystery, lest you should be wise in your own opinion, that blindness in part has happened to Israel until the fullness of the Gentiles has come in. 26 And so all Israel will be saved, as it is written: "The Deliverer will come out of Zion, And He will turn away ungodliness from Jacob; Romans 11:25-26

The testimony of the fourth recipients did not fail to materialise, your miracles will come to pass. Let's turn to the fifth receiver.

Bartimaeus, The Mercy Crier—(Mark 10:46-52; Luke 18:35-43)

> 46 Now they came to Jericho. As He went out of Jericho with His disciples and a great multitude, blind Bartimaeus, the son of Timaeus, sat by the road begging. 47 And when he heard that it was Jesus of Nazareth, he began to cry out and say, "Jesus, Son of David, have mercy on me!" 48 Then many warned him to be quiet; but he cried out all the more, "Son of David, have mercy on me!" 49 So Jesus stood still and commanded him to be called. Then they called the blind man, saying to him, "Be of good cheer. Rise, He is calling you." 50 And throwing aside his garment, he rose and came to Jesus. 51 So Jesus answered and said to him, "What do you

---

20   William MacDonald, (Editor, Art Farstad), Believer's Bible Commentary, London: Thomas Nelson Publishers, 1995, p. 1280

want Me to do for you?" The blind man said to Him, "Rabboni, that I may receive my sight." 52 Then Jesus said to him, "Go your way; your faith has made you well." And immediately he received his sight and followed Jesus on the road. Mark 10:47-52

When talking about one of the fortunate individuals who received a direct response in regards to a prayer for mercy, Bartimaeus' case was a unique one. His prayer for compassion from Jesus was heard and his life changed completely. The opposition was obvious and stern, yet, he was resolute in his decision to get answers. You will not be locked out by the opposition at the time of your visitation.

Further, it was a desperate situation which needed a desperate solution, as I said earlier in one of the chapters in this book. Although, he lacked a physical sight, but he had an insightful revelation of who Jesus was, He called Him, 'Thou Son of David'. The implication of that remark is massive, because it brings one to the point of Jesus' genealogical root (Matthew 1:5-6, 16), and scripture has already testified that the Messiah would be a descendant of King David (Isaiah 9:7).

Furthermore, by calling Jesus by that reference, he wanted Jesus to know that, he (Bartimaeus) believed on Him as the Messiah as was predicted, whereas others were following out of curiosity, or because of Jesus' fame, partly due to the miracles He had done at some other places.

Ironically, it seems that the nation of Israel was blind to the presence of the Messiah during that time, but Bartimaeus had true spiritual sight.[21] Do not be surprised that presently,

---

21 William MacDonald, (Editor, Art Farstad), Believer's Bible Commentary, London: Thomas Nelson Publishers, 1995, p. 1349

some people are blind to the presence of Jesus Christ, same as the days of old Israel—a browse on the internet and you will hear all kinds of stories about Jesus and His followers.

Notwithstanding, the next most important event at this time is the granting of the prayers for mercy by the roadside, not in the synagogue, temple, church, or on a crusade ground. The conclusion of the story of the fifth recipient in this section is that, the blind man was healed of his crippling disease. Call on His name wherever you are, and Jesus will answer you. The sixth recipients below were aged parents, namely, Zacharias and Elizabeth, (Luke 1:24-25). The story of the elderly couples suggests that age cannot be a barrier to receiving mercy.

God Shows Mercy On Those Who Fear Him, (Luke 1:50-58)

And His mercy is on those who fear Him, From generation to generation. 51 He has shown strength with His arm; He has scattered the proud in the imagination of their hearts. 52 He has put down the mighty from their thrones, And exalted the lowly. 53 He has filled the hungry with good things, And the rich He has sent away empty. 54 He has helped His servant Israel, In remembrance of His mercy, 55 As He spoke to our fathers, To Abraham and to his seed forever." 56 And Mary remained with her about three months, and returned to her house. 57 Now Elizabeth's full time came for her to be delivered, and she brought forth a son. 58 When her neighbors and relatives heard how the Lord had shown great mercy to her, they rejoiced with her. Luke 1:50-58

I was thinking that because of slander and suspicion that, the neighbours had about Mary and her pregnancy, she wouldn't be patient for God to finish His work in her life. But think about it, the same way in which God chose Mary to be the mother of the Saviour, He could have chosen any of us to be a pioneer of a project. Are you the understanding type? Are you willing to co-operate with God, and will you allow Him to use you? As it happened, Mary disappointed all her critics when she obeyed God, (Luke 1:38).

> 38 Then Mary said, "Behold the maidservant of the Lord! Let it be to me according to your word." And the angel departed from her. Luke 1:38

Observe that because of the earlier remarks (Luke 1:50-58) which were credited to Mary, some of the lessons we can learn are:

- Humility, that is, learn to be humble.
- Celebrate God's faithfulness throughout your generation.
- Praise God for His mercy towards yourself.
- Appreciate God for who He is.

The seventh receiver of mercy below, was a victim of robbery. He almost died but mercy found him. May mercy be available to you always.

The Robbery Victim, (The Good Samaritan) Luke 10:30-37

> 30 Then Jesus answered and said: "A certain man went down from Jerusalem to Jericho, and fell among thieves, who stripped him of his clothing, wounded him, and departed, leaving him half dead. 31 Now by chance a certain priest came down that road. And when he saw him, he passed by on the other side. 32

Likewise a Levite, when he arrived at the place, came and looked, and passed by on the other side. 33 But a certain Samaritan, as he journeyed, came where he was. And when he saw him, he had compassion. 34 So he went to him and bandaged his wounds, pouring on oil and wine; and he set him on his own animal, brought him to an inn, and took care of him. 35 On the next day, when he departed, he took out two denarii, gave them to the innkeeper, and said to him, 'Take care of him; and whatever more you spend, when I come again, I will repay you.' 36 So which of these three do you think was neighbor to him who fell among the thieves?" 37 And he said, "He who showed mercy on him." Luke 10:30-37

The illustration before us is that of an individual who was robbed due to no fault of his. The setting (the road from Jerusalem to Jericho was nineteen miles at the time), was rocky, desolate, and a notorious area which was prone to robbery in real life.[22] Presumptively, it could be that the wounded man was on a business trip when the incident happened. Or, someone going to work, for job-hunt, drop off their children at school, attending church, etc.

Without any doubt, the wounded man was vulnerable at that period of time, and before help was available, the bandits pounced on him and nearly killed him. The robbers took advantage of him at a time when assistance was far away. Believers wake up! Your enemy like a roaring lion is looking for someone to devour, (1 Peter 5:8). Don't be careless.

---

22 Jamieson, Fausset and Brown, Commentary On The Whole Bible, Grand Rapids, Michigan: Zondervan Publishing House, 1961, p. 1004

May God's help and assistance be available to you constantly. Unfortunately, the wounded man was powerless and too weak to confront, fight and defeat his opponents when the attack occurred. It has been said, "If you faint in the day of adversity, Your strength is small," (Proverbs 24:10). May your strength not fail you on your day of attack. But, note that, without God's help, we cannot fight the enemy and earn victory.

Sad to say, but the truth is that, many people have been robbed, denied, bruised and violated in today's world by the devil. They need to be healed, we all do. Obviously, many of us have been left disappointed some time in our lives before. Imagine the instances where those we trusted to help, didn't. Instead they turned their eyes the other way—the 'priests' and the 'levites' of this world (as in the story of the Good Samaritan), are good reminders.

It is surprising that help came for the robbery victim (a Jew, whose fellows didn't stop to help him), from where no one expected—a Samaritan? Originally, the Samaritans were the mixed race that the Jews would not associate themselves, (John 4:9). Listen to what the woman at the well said to Jesus,

> 9 Then the woman of Samaria said to Him, "How is it that You, being a Jew, ask a drink from me, a Samaritan woman?" For Jews have no dealings with Samaritans. John 4:9

What a frank talk! However, the Samaritan in the text showed love and was compassionate, and did not treat the accident victim the way the Jews would normally treat the Samaritans. May mercy cause you to be helped. What can we learn from the story? Moral lessons from the story include:

- Don't encourage racial bias and cultural discrimination because God created every person.
- Never think like the Jews who thought they were better than the Samaritans.
- Be kind to people, be thoughtful in your actions, be loving and helpful to people.
- Remember Jesus' teaching where He said, "Blessed are the merciful for they shall obtain mercy," (Matthew 5:7).
- Be merciful and compassionate like the Samaritan in the above scripture, because it is possible to identify the Samaritan with Jesus who came to rescue us from the devil and has made provision for us from this earth to heaven and through all eternity.[23]

This God who has been consistent in showing mercy up to the seventh recipient, is progressing to the eighth recipient below. They are lepers, the rejects in society, yet, the Creator could accommodate them. Are you surprised? Don't be, because your time has come.

Ten Men Appeal For Compassion, (Luke 17:11-14)

The ten lepers with their skin disease had a Religious Restriction Order (RRO), imposed on them by their Hebrew community which must not be violated by any person suffering the condition. So, they kept their distance to avoid breaking the law, they were unclean and must not cause others to become unclean. In the name of the Lord, let all satanic restriction order be destroyed for you. Let us read (Luke 17:11-14),

11 Now it happened as He went to Jerusalem that He passed through the midst of Samaria and Galilee.

23 William MacDonald, (Editor, Art Farstad), Believer's Bible Commentary, London: Thomas Nelson Publishers, 1995, p. 1410

12 Then as He entered a certain village, there met Him ten men who were lepers, who stood afar off. 13 And they lifted up their voices and said, "Jesus, Master, have mercy on us!" 14 So when He saw them, He said to them, "Go, show yourselves to the priests." And so it was that as they went, they were cleansed. Luke 17:11-14

Apart from the imposition of the RRO above, the ten lepers had to keep away to prevent the infection from spreading, and to avoid incurring the anger of the public who gave them alms. You can imagine the extent of dilemma the ten men had to bear daily. May everything and anything that can keep you away from reaching your goals in life be destroyed in the name of Jesus Christ.

Interestingly, the ten lepers were not prohibited from crying out to the Lord who was on His last journey to Jerusalem before His crucifixion. It isn't the same in comparison but allow me to use this example. Let us assume that you were travelling home for your Christmas break, and your flight was the last one for the year, and there is no other means of transportation for you to get home, would you not be desperate to catch the flight by all means? So, out of their despair the ten lepers cried as loud as they could.

The lepers raising their voices suggest that there will always be a way to attract God's attention, provided you can look beyond the problem. As recorded by the physician writer, the ten lepers acted in faith, hinged their request on the mercy of God, and Jesus was compassionate towards them. One of the moral lessons here is that, God's mercy is for everybody. God's mercy is available to you, ask for yours, for as many who ask, they receive, Matthew 7:7-8

7 "Ask, and it will be given to you; seek, and you will find; knock, and it will be opened to you. 8 For everyone who asks receives, and he who seeks finds, and to him who knocks it will be opened. Matthew 7:7-8

Note that, the ten lepers had a life-changing disease which secluded them from their society, but through God's compassion they were healed, restored back to the community and they no longer depended on alms and stipends collected from their good neighbours. Who has shunned you? Have you been ignored because of a challenge? Have people turned their back against your marriage, business, ministry, career and so on? God can be merciful to you too. Ask Jesus to have mercy on you like the ten men. Yes, Jesus will have mercy on you, ask him. God even cares about your basic needs. See how He attended to the ninth receivers below and be encouraged.

Jesus Cares About Our Basic Needs (Matthew 15:32-38)

There were no Food Banks or Humanitarian Aid Centres to resort to. People were hungry for food and Jesus was able to sense that. Would this Man of Galilee ignore the appeal for food in the eyes of the multitudes? His words to His disciples were full of compassion and love. He said, "I have compassion on the multitude, because they have now continued with Me three days and have nothing to eat. And I do not want to send them away hungry, lest they faint on the way." The One who was concerned about their hunger for food, can identify with your lack. Let us read the full text, (Matthew 15:32-38),

32 Now Jesus called His disciples to Himself and said, "I have compassion on the multitude, because they

have now continued with Me three days and have nothing to eat. And I do not want to send them away hungry, lest they faint on the way." 33 Then His disciples said to Him, "Where could we get enough bread in the wilderness to fill such a great multitude?" 34 Jesus said to them, "How many loaves do you have?" And they said, "Seven, and a few little fish." 35 So He commanded the multitude to sit down on the ground. 36 And He took the seven loaves and the fish and gave thanks, broke them and gave them to His disciples; and the disciples gave to the multitude. 37 So they all ate and were filled, and they took up seven large baskets full of the fragments that were left. 38 Now those who ate were four thousand men, besides women and children. Matthew 15:32-38

The devil had thought Jesus would neglect the physical needs of His immediate audience at the time, but the devil was proved wrong. Would God who fed the multitudes in (Exodus 16:34-35) for forty years forget to feed the crowd who had followed Him for three days?

34 As the LORD commanded Moses, so Aaron laid it up before the Testimony, to be kept. 35 And the children of Israel ate manna forty years, until they came to an inhabited land; they ate manna until they came to the border of the land of Canaan. Exodus 16:34-35

Would the One who fed five thousand people in (Matthew 14:16-21), excluding women and children not be able to do it again, if so required? The aforementioned are some of the evidences of what the Saviour can do. There is nothing God cannot do out of compassion. Be ready for your miracles through His mercy, love and compassion.

Sorrow Turned To Joy For The Widow At Nain, (Luke 7:11-15)

Would that be deemed as a mere coincidence, drama, or a rehearsed play? None of that. Nain was was a little village south of Nazareth where Jesus met the widow who was in a funeral procession with a large crowd following her, because her only son was dead. The Life-giving Saviour touched the open coffin and raised the dead young man, and so turned their mourning into dancing. The only explainable rationale behind this act was compassion. Let us read the full story, (Luke 7:11-15),

> 11 Now it happened, the day after, that He went into a city called Nain; and many of His disciples went with Him, and a large crowd. 12 And when He came near the gate of the city, behold, a dead man was being carried out, the only son of his mother; and she was a widow. And a large crowd from the city was with her. 13 When the Lord saw her, He had compassion on her and said to her, "Do not weep." 14 Then He came and touched the open coffin, and those who carried him stood still. And He said, "Young man, I say to you, arise." 15 So he who was dead sat up and began to speak. And He presented him to his mother. Luke 7:11-15

The Jewish Rabbi knew the implication of what He was doing because by touching a dead body, Jesus would be religiously unclean as was the custom of the Jews at the time. Why did He do that? Jesus did that because, He is Lord over death and disease. Also, because He had compassion on the widow whose only son supporting her was dead. May God be merciful to you. You will not lose your supporters (financial, material, marital, ministry and business) in the name of Jesus Christ.

Note, "And when He (Jesus) came near the gate of the city, behold, a dead man was being carried out," What a timely divine co-incidence! It does not matter how close you are to being disgraced, disappointed, rejected, and refused, as it was never too late for the widow at Nain, your case will not be too late, nor difficult for God to handle. I pray for you that there will be a timely divine co-incidence for you starting from now. Hear me, from the first selected recipient to the tenth as provided above, God did not fail. He will not fail you. May you, your family, business, career, ministry and whatever you lay your hands to do as God's child, fetch you miracles in the name of Jesus Christ. Amen.

BOOKS BY THE AUTHOR

101 REASONS WHY PEOPLE FAIL IN LEADERSHIP

THE AMBASSADOR'S MIRROR

FORGIVE & FORGET: GOD'S LOVE TOWARDS MANKIND

THE NATURE OF GRACE: REDEMPTION FOR UNDESERVING HUMANITY BEYOND NOAHIC TIME

PRAYER RAIN: AN ESSENTIAL MASTER-KEY FOR CHRISTIAN PILGRIMS FOR RETREAT & THE HOLY LAND

THE UNIVERSALITY OF GOD'S MERCIES: THE BOOK OF JONAH

BIBLIOGRAPHY

Ajibolorunrin, I. O., *Prayer Rain: An Essential Master-key for Christian Pilgrims for Retreat & The Holy Land*, (London: Grosvenor House Publishing Limited, 2023)

Clines, D. J. A., Writing on Job in D. A. Carson, et al, (Consulting ed.), *New Bible Commentary 21st Century Edition*, (Leicester, England: Inter-Varsity Press, 1994)

Collins, G. R., *Christian Counselling: A Comprehensive Guide, Revised Edition*, (London: Word Publishing, 1988)

France, R. T., *Contribution on Matthew in New Bible Commentary, 21st Century Edition*, (Leicester, England: Inter-Varsity Press, 1994)

Jamieson, R., Fausset, A. R., Brown, D., *Commentary On the Whole Bible*, (Grand Rapids, Michigan: Zondervan Publishing House, 1961)

Kitchen, K. A., Writing on Egypt in David and Pat Alexander, *The Lion Handbook to the Bible*, (Oxford, England: Lion Publishing plc, 1983)

MacDonald, W., Farstad, A., (Ed.), *Believer's Bible Commentary—A Complete Bible Commentary in One Volume*, (London: Thomas Nelson Publishers, 1995)

Stigers H., Writing on 2 Kings in Charles F. Pfeiffer, *The Wycliffe Bible Commentary*, (Chicago: Moody Press, 1962)

Stuart, D., Writing on the Book of Jonah in *New Bible Commentary, 21st Century Edition*, (Leicester, England: Inter-Varsity Press, 1994)

Taylor, M. D., *The Complete Book of Bible Literacy*, (Wheaton, Illinois: Tyndale House Publishers, 1992)

Williams, W., (Ed.,), *New Concise Bible Dictionary*, (Leicester, England: Inter-Varsity Press, 1989)

Yates, K. M., Writing on The Book of Psalms in Charles F. Pfeiffer, (Ed.,), *The Wycliffe Bible Commentary*, (Chicago: Moody Press, 1962)

Bibles

Authorized (King James) Version (AV)

Newspaper

The Punch. (Ikeja, Lagos State, Nigeria), March 14, 2015

Websites

https://www.biblegateway.com

www.britannica.com/place/Nineveh. Cited on 12/07/2024